Classical Monologues

A collection of monologues for female actors

Compiled & edited by Kim Gilbert

ISBN: 9798673212233

DEDICATION

This collection of Classical monologues for female actors is dedicated to all teachers and students of drama. There is a varied selection of dramatic scenes dating from the Greeks, Shakespeare, Restoration Drama, Realism, The Victorians as well as several foreign dramatists. I hope you gain as much satisfaction from these writings as I have.

ACKNOWLEDGEMENTS

A special thanks goes to my husband, Steve, who has prepared this book for publication. He has bailed me out on numerous occasions over the years with his technical expertise.

TABLE OF CONTENTS

Classical Monologues for Female Actors

INTRODUCTION

I have compiled and edited this collection of classical monologues for female actors to study as well as enjoy. These classic scenes are suitable for a range of solo acting exams as well as for auditions and festivals. This book is ideal for students and is a useful resource study for teachers of drama. I have tried and tested these scenes with numerous students over the years with great success and more importantly, they have thoroughly enjoyed working on them.

The monologues in this collection are taken from a range of classical drama ranging from some of the finest Greek playwrights to works from the 18th, 19th and early 20th Centuries. There are some notes about the period and style of writing, along with some acting tips. Each scene has an introduction prepared suitable for exam or festival work and are also timed with exams and festival work in mind. I hope you enjoy this collection.

Classical Monologues for Female Actors

THE GREEK PLAYS

EURIPIDES

ARISTOPHANES

SOPHOCLES

Classical Monologues for Female Actors

Classical Monologues for Female Actors

4

ANCIENT GREEK THEATRE & LITERATURE

The Greek Empire began in the 8th Century BC and fell in the 4th Century BC. It was during this period that theatre originated. Ancient Greek theatre flourished, and from this, three genres emerged, tragedy, which emerged during the late 6th century BC, comedy, 486 BC and the satyr play. Theatre developed from a festival during the grape harvesting time, which the Greeks celebrated in honour of the God Dionysus. This eventually turned into a playwriting competition, and it was for festivals like these that most of the Ancient literature we have today was written for. Theatre was extremely important in Ancient Greek Civilisation. To signify the importance of this event, the high status Olympic Champions, were given the privilege of the best seats in the theatre. The sheer size of the open air amphitheatres is extraordinary, some holding 15,000 people. These theatres were either semi-circular or entirely circular, providing fantastic acoustics. There was an orchestra, where the Chorus usually stood, and a skene which was a backdrop and was also a place for the actors to change. Little is known about the acting styles in Greek theatre. There was no fourth wall. Like the chorus, the actors could see the audience, and would have spoken directly to them. The actors' masks were quite sophisticated and had megaphones built into the mouths of their masks to amplify their voices.

Greece's poetic movement was one of the key literary movements of Ancient Greece during the period between the 7th and 4th centuries BC. It was during this movement that poetry was being written down for the first time, and in many forms, for example, the ode, epic, tragedy, comedy, therefore making this one of the greatest and revolutionary movements in world history. It ended when Greece was conquered by Rome, and the Republican period began.

Ancient theatre is known for the wearing of masks and allowed those seated at the back of the theatre to see the expressions of the characters. This therefore meant that the audience knew the characters' age, sex, status and also how they should react and respond towards the characters. For the Chorus of the play, the masks created unity, representing a many-voiced persona. Just like group speaking today. Furthermore, masks allowed the all-male cast to play female characters convincingly, while also heightening the emotions of the audience. This use of masks has inspired many modern theatre styles, particularly Commedia dell Arte, which relies on physical movement and masks to portray the characters to the audience.

The Ancient Greeks wore long flowing tunics and boots called *cothurni*, worn by those playing tragic roles. These boots elevated them above the other actors. The actors with comedic roles only wore a thin-soled shoe called a sock. These both clearly symbolized the roles of each actor, whilst also ensuring the audience members at the back of the theatre could follow the plot, by visually representing the mood of each scene.

The Chorus, a common part of an Ancient play, consisted of between 12 and 50 players, Aeschylus lowered the number to twelve, and Sophocles raised it again to fifteen. The group was led by the choryphaeus who was the main member of the Chorus. They often danced, sang and spoke their lines in unison, commenting on the action of the performance. They helped to offer context and summarized the performance.

Most Ancient poetry or prose is written in dactylic hexameter. This rhythm consists of one long syllable followed by two shorter syllables, having the rhythm **dum** de de/**dum** de de/**dum** de de/ **dum** de de/**dum** de de/**dum** de de. Hexameter indicates that this rhythm is repeated six times per line. The translations of the Ancient literature which we read now-a-days, no longer has this rhythm. It is often translated into prose. The Ancient drama dialogue is written in iambic trimeter, which consists of one stressed syllable followed by one unstressed syllable, **dum** de/**dum** de/**dum** de. Trimeter means that this is repeated three times per line. The Chorus' lines are instead written in choral lyric, suggesting that they were sung instead of spoken.

Euripides

Euripides was a Greek playwright living between 480-406 BC.
Euripides is known as one of the three greatest tragedians, along
with Aeschylus and Sophocles. Although he has this title today, he
was unappreciated during his life, winning just four awards, in
comparison to Sophocles' twenty. This is because Euripides was
known as a leader of 'corrupt views', challenging the state with his
writing. He and many others competed in the dramatic festival of
Dionysus, and it was here where Euripides was ridiculed. The
comic playwright, Aristophanes, scripted Euripides as a foolish
character in three of his plays, publicly humiliating him. Euripides
was a rather eccentric man, having been married twice, yet both
wives having been unfaithful. He became a recluse, and lived in a
cave on the island of Salamis. Despite this, Euripides influenced
modern theatre drastically, as he represented mythical heroes as
ordinary people in extraordinary circumstances. He therefore
became known as 'the most tragic of poets' as he focused on the
inner lives and motives of characters, adding more depth to the
stock two-dimensional characters of myths. Euripides' most
famous works include *Medea*, *Trojan Women* and *The Bacchae*.
Medea was rather unpopular at the time, due to his inclusions of
dragons, which was considered untraditional and ridiculous.
Furthermore, Euripides portrays the character of Medea as
sympathetic whereas Jason appears cowardly. This would have
been unpopular among his contemporary audiences which
consisted mostly of men.

Aristophanes

Aristophanes lived between 446 and 386 BC, Aristophanes was a
comic playwright from Athens, known as the 'Father of Comedy'.
Eleven of his thirty plays have survived complete, and it is these
plays which are used to define the genre Old Comedy.
Aristophanes' powers of ridicule were acknowledged and feared
by many, including Plato who stated that Aristophanes' play *The
Clouds* contributed to the trial and later execution of Socrates.
Aristophanes also caricatured influential statesmen such as
Cleon, and the playwright Euripides, mocking them. Most of what
we know about Aristophanes comes from the study of his plays,

as it was common in Old Comedy for the Chorus to speak the opinion of the author. His play *Lysistrata* was originally performed in Athens in 411BC, and is a comical account of one woman's effort to end the Peloponnesian War by persuading Greek women to refrain from sexual intercourse with their husbands, forcing them to negotiate peace. It is here where Aristophanes can be likened to Euripides, as they both portray strong female characters, quite uncommon in Ancient literature. Lysistrata can be described as an early feminist, as women of the Ancient world were encouraged not to speak their minds unless given permission by their husbands. Yet Lysistrata completely disregards this and becomes a spokesperson, sharing her strong opinions and encouraging others to join her cause, much like a politician. Quite remarkable in such times.

Sophocles

Sophocles lived between the years 496 and 406 BC, Sophocles remains one of the greatest influencers of drama. An example of his innovations is his addition of a third actor, which further reduced the role of the chorus and created greater opportunity for character development and conflict between characters. This was an interest of Sophocles', as he was more concerned with a characters' struggle with fate and character development. Sophocles won more competitions than both of his contemporary tragic writers, enjoying a total of at least 18 wins. It is thought that Sophocles wrote at least 123 plays, only 7 of which have survived, the most famous being *Antigone, Oedipus Rex* and *Ajax. Antigone* and *Oedipus Rex* are part of a trilogy following the misfortunes of King Oedipus who married his mother, and upon discovering the truth, blinded himself. *Antigone* focuses on the fate of his daughter after his death, as she is faced with the choice of obeying the law of the king of the land and leave her brother's body to remain unburied, or to obey the law of the gods. She decides to bury her brother, and is, as a result, sentenced to death. The complex concepts of right and wrong, punishment and reward are present throughout Sophocles' writing, indicating that the choices made by characters were of interest to him.

ELECTRA by EURIPIDES (410 BC)

(Electra and her brother, Orestes, take revenge on their mother, Clytemnestra. Clytemnestra murdered their father, Agamemnon, and has now taken another lover, Aegisthus, casting out Electra and Orestes. Electra is now married to a farmer. In this scene, her resentment towards her mother is very powerful. Electra is talking to her long-lost brother who appears as a 'stranger'. She pleads with him to find her brother. Once, the two siblings recognize each other, they plot their revenge to kill the usurper, Aegisthus).

Electra:

I will tell it I must – and must tell you who love me –
How my luck, and my father's, is too heavy to lift.
Since you have moved me to speak so, stranger, I must beg
That you will tell Orestes all my distress, and his.
First tell him how I am kept like a beast in stable rags,
My skin heavy with grease and dirt. Describe to him
This hut – my home, who used to live in the king's palace.
I weave my clothes myself and slave-like at the loom,
Must work or else walk naked through the world in nothing.
I fetch and carry water from the riverside,
I am deprived of holy festivals and dances,
I cannot talk to women since I am a girl,
I cannot think of Castor, who was close in blood
And loved me once, before he rose among the gods.
My mother in the glory of her Phrygian rugs
Sits on the throne, while circled at her feet the girls
Of Asia stoop, whom Father won at the sack of Troy,
Their clothes woven in snowy wood from Ida, pinned
With golden brooches, while the walls and floor are stained
Still with my father's black and rotting blood. The man
Who murdered him goes riding grand in Father's chariot,
With bloody hands and high delight lifting the staff
Of office by which Father marshalled the Greek lords.
The tomb of Agamemnon finds no honor yet,
Never yet drenched with holy liquids or made green
In myrtle branches, barren of bright sacrifice.
But in his drunken fits, my mother's lover, brilliant

Man, triumphant leaps and dances on the mound
Or pelts my father's stone memorial with rocks
And dares to shout against us with his boldened tongue:
"Where is your son, Orestes? When will that noble youth
Come to protect your tomb?" Insults to empty space.
Kind stranger, as I ask you, tell him all these things.
For many call him home again – I speak for them –
The voices in our hands and tongues and grieving minds
And heads, shaven in mourning; and his father calls.
All will be shamed if he whose father captured Troy
Cannot in single courage kill a single man,
Although his strength is younger and his blood more noble.

THE WOMEN OF TROY by EURIPIDES 415 BC

(*This play is also known as The Trojan Women. Cassandra is the eldest daughter of Priam and Hecuba. Many believe her to be insane, or psychic. The Trojan women have suffered after the city of Troy has been attacked and the men killed. Those remaining have been taken as slaves. Cassandra seeks revenge on those who killed her family. This scene comes from the beginning of the play*).

Cassandra:

Put a garland of victory on my head, Mother, and rejoice at my royal marriage! Take me to Agamemnon; if you find me reluctant, force me; for if Apollo is a god, this famous king of Greeks will find me a more fatal bride than Helen was. I shall be his death, and the ruin of his whole house; so, I shall avenge my brothers and my father.

Enough of that; I will not prophesy of the axe that shall fall on my neck – and not only on mine; or of the agony that shall follow from my marriage, when son murders mother; or of the overthrow of the dynasty of Atreus. Yes, there is a god possesses me – but this at least is no mad raving: I will show you that this Troy of ours is more enviable than Greece! Greece for the sake of one woman – and her lust – went hunting Helen and led ten thousand men to death! Yes – enough of Odysseus: those arrows are not yet shot. Lead on! My bridegroom is waiting for me at the porch of death! You have lived with a curse – with a curse they shall bury you, secretly,
In the night – pale shadow of Majesty, prime commander of Greece!
Near your dishonoured grave they will fling my naked body
Out where wintry floods course down the mountain chasms,
And beasts will pick the bones of Apollo's virgin priestess.
Go, garland of Phoebus, symbol of dear devotion.
Go with the vanished joys of his temple-celebrations,
Go, his gifts – I tear you from my still untainted body
For the swift winds to carry back to the Lord of Prophecy!
Where is the ship? Which is the way? Lose not a moment, watch

For the wind stirring the sails! You are sending me to Hellas
As one of three Avengers. Mother, no tears! Farewell!
Oh, my brothers, buried in this dear earth of Troy,
My father, you have not long to wait for me. I will come
To the House of Death triumphant, my hands and garments red
With the blood of the House of Atreus, who brought out Troy to
dust!

ANDROMACHE by EURIPIDES 425BC

(Andromache is at the temple of Thetis. She is clinging to the altar. Andromache now leads the life of a slave. She is in conflict with her master's new wife, Hermione. In this scene, she is mourning her plight and also her dead husband, Hector).

Andromache:

O city of Thebes, glory of Asia, whence on a day I came to Priam's princely home with many a rich and costly thing in my dower, affianced unto Hector to be the mother of his children, I Andromache, envied name in days of yore, but now of all women that have been or yet shall be the most unfortunate; for I have lived to see my husband Hector slain by Achilles, and the babe Astyanax, whom I bore my lord, hurled from the towering battlements, when the Hellenes sacked our Trojan home; and I myself am come to Hellas as a slave, though I was esteemed a daughter of a race most free, given to Neoptolemus that island-prince, and set apart for him as his special prize from the spoils of Troy. And here I dwell upon the boundaries of Phthia and Pharsalia's town, where Thetis erst, the goddess of the sea, abode with Peleus apart from the world, avoiding the throng of men; wherefore the folk of Thessaly call it the sacred place of Thetis, in honour of the goddess's marriage. Here dwells the son of Achilles and suffers Peleus still to rule Pharsalia, not wishing to assume the sceptre while the old man lives. Within these halls have borne a boy to the son of Achilles, my master. Now aforetime for all my misery I ever had a hope to lead me on, that, if my child were safe, I might find some help and protection from my woes; but since my lord in scorn of his bondmaid's charms hath wedded that Spartan Hermione, I am tormented by her most cruelly; for she saith that I by secret enchantment am making her barren and distasteful to her husband, and that I design to take her place in this house, ousting her the rightful mistress by force; whereas I at first submitted against my will and now have resigned my place; be almighty Zeus my witness that it was not of my own free will I became her rival!

But I cannot convince her, and she longs to kill me, and her father Menelaus is an accomplice in this. E'en now is he within, arrived from Sparta for this very purpose, while I in terror am come to take up position here in the shrine of Thetis adjoining the house, if haply it may save me from death; for Peleus and his descendants hold it in honour as symbol of his marriage with the Nereid. My only son am I secretly conveying to a neighbour's house in fear for his life. For his sire stands not by my side to lend his aid and cannot avail his child at all, being absent in the land of Delphi, where he is offering recompense to Loxias for the madness he committed, when on a day he went to Pytho and demanded of Phoebus satisfaction for his father's death, if haply his prayer might avert those past sins and win for him the god's goodwill hereafter.

MEDEA by EURIPIDES 431BC

(Medea's husband has taken a new wife and Medea is to be sent away. She is naturally outraged and addresses Jason, at first with anger and later in the scene, with cunning in order to achieve her plans. She later poisons Jason's new wife along with her beloved sons).

Medea:

You come to us, where you're most hated, here?
Is this your courage and heroic boldness.
To wrong your friends, then look them in the face?
No: it's that worst disease of human minds,
A blank where shame should be. But I am glad you came;
It makes my heart a little easier
To spear you with my words, and watch you writhe.

I'll begin at the beginning.
I saved your life, as every Greek can witness
Who joined you in the voyage of the Argo;
(I helped you catch the fire-breathing oxen
And harness them, and sow the fatal field;)
I killed the dragon, the sleepless sentinel
That wound its coils around the Golden Fleece;
I held the light of safety over you.
I chose to desert my father and my home
To come with you to Iolcos; full of love,
Empty of thought, in those days. After that, I killed
King Pelias, using his own daughters' hands
For the unkindest death, to wipe his blood-line out.
I did all that for you, and now you drop me;
You take a new wife, seeming to forget
That we have children. If you were a childless man,
One might forgive your lusting for her bed …
But all your oaths and promises are broken:
I cannot trust you now. Nor can I understand
What you believe in – do you think the gods
That used to govern us no longer do?
You seem to imagine the moral law has changed –

15

But even you must realize you've not kept your word.
Look at this hand you took in yours so often
These knees you clung to, begging me to help:
The meaningless embraces of a bad
Husband! The hopes I entertained and lost!
Come on! I shall confide in you, like some old friend-
There's nothing I can gain from you, I know that,
But still – I can expose your shame with questions:
Where can I turn to, now? Home to my father?
I betrayed my home and country to come with you.
To the grieving daughters of King Pelias?
A fine welcome they'd give me
In the house where I killed their father.
It comes to this: the friends I had at home
Now hate me; and in other places too
Where I need not have harmed a soul, I did,
Because you asked me to. They hate me now as well.
So, in return for that, you made me 'happy' –
Greek women think so, anyway: 'What a wonderful
And faithful man that lucky woman has!'
This husband who calmly lets me go, to exile,
Without a friend, alone with fatherless children –
A fine beginning for a newly-married man,
That his children and the woman who saved his life
Must wander abroad in cringing beggary.

Oh Zeus, why did you give humanity
The clearest evidence when gold is false –
But set no markings on the skin of man
To single out the bad one from the good?

LYSISTRATA by ARISTOPHANES 411BC

(Lysistrata wishes to end the Peloponnesian War. She gathers the women from local areas and insists that the only way to stop their warring husbands is by denying their husband's sex until they promise to sign a Peace treaty. Meanwhile, the older women are told to seize the Acropolis).

Lysistrata:

Oh, Calnice, my heart is on fire; I blush for our sex. Men will have it we are tricky and sly …

Yet, look you, when the women are summoned to meet for a matter of the last importance, they lie abed instead of coming.

But I tell you the business that calls them here is far and away more urgent.

A big affair. Both big and great. It concerns a thing I have turned about and about this way and that of many sleepless nights.

So fine, it means just this, Greece saved by the women!

Our country's fortunes depend on us – it is with us to undo utterly the Peloponnesians. To exterminate the Boetians to a man!
For Athen's sake, I will never threaten so fell a doom; trust me for that. However, if the Boetian and Peloponnesian women join us, Greece is saved.

These are the very sheet-anchors of our salvation – these yellow tunics, these scents and slippers, these cosmetics and transparent robes. There is not a man will wield a lance against another … or want a shield … or draw a sword.

I have discovered a means of ending the War, will you all second me?

Then I will out with it at last, my mighty secret! Oh! Sister women, if we would compel our husbands to make peace, we must refrain

… we must refrain from the male altogether … Nay, why do you turn your backs on me? Where are you going? So, you bite your lips, and shake your heads, eh? Why these pale, sad looks? Why these tears? Come, will you do it – yes or no? Do you hesitate?

Oh, wanton, vicious sex! The poets have done well to make tragedies upon us; we are good for nothing then but love and lewdness! We need only sit indoors with painted cheeks, and meet our mates lightly clad in transparent gowns of Amorgos silk, and employing all our charms and all our arts; then they will act like mad and they will be wild to lie with us. That will be the time to refuse, and they will hasten to make peace, I am convinced of that!

There are a thousand ways of tormenting them. Never fear, they'll soon tire of the game; there's no satisfaction for a man, unless the woman shares it. Have no fear; we undertake to make our own people hear reason. This very day the Acropolis will be in our hands. That is the task assigned to the older women; while we are here in council, they are going, under pretence of offering sacrifice, to seize the citadel. Come, quick, and let us bind ourselves by an inviolable oath.

ANTIGONE by SOPHOCLES (442 BC)

(Antigone is talking to her uncle, King Creon. She is determined to bury her brother at any cost even if the price to pay, is with her life).

Antigone:

Yes. It wasn't the law of Zeus I broke.
Your decree laughs in the face of justice.
It's perfectly simple: you have no right
To pass such laws. You're just a little man,
And you will die. How can you overturn
The great enduring laws of the immortals?
You can't rewrite them when you feel like it!
For yesterday, tomorrow and today
Dissolve within the greatness of their will.
There's nothing brave in standing up to you.
I'm far too scared to break my Gods' laws.
Of course, I knew that you'd put me to death:
It really doesn't need and sham decree,
It doesn't matter so much when I die,
The sooner the better in fact. My pain
Is as wide as the sea; I want to die.
I do not want to see my mother's son
Stretched naked in the field and his white flesh
Pulled at by dogs. That I could not endure.
Do you think I'm a fool, Creon? Perhaps.
But then fools see fools everywhere, don't they?
Are you sure killing me will be enough?
Then why put it off? You go on and on:
It hurts my ears; and what I say hurts you.
What greater glory could I ever know
Than when I lay my brother in the grave?
These men here, they see me, they admire me,
But don't worry, they won't say anything.
They're scared of you. It must be nice to be
A King – you can get away with murder.
These men see what I see but shut their mouths for you.
I was not born to separate in hate.

My mother gave me life to join in love.

SHAKESPEARE

ELIZABETHAN DRAMATIST
1564-1616

SHAKESPEARE'S WRITING STYLE

During the Elizabethan times, there were no female actresses, only male actors. The young boys played the women's parts. The actors were given only their own parts to the play. It wasn't until the 16th and 17th Century that printing became available, enabling Shakespeare's plays to be published. Printers would often change the words of a playwright's play in order for them to fit onto the published page. Shakespeare's characters are depicted as real people with universal emotions. However, one must appreciate the writing is most often in verse and therefore knowledge of the metre and style of his writing is essential.

Metre and Rhythm

English is a stress language. This means that our language is made up of strong and weak stresses. Verse is made up of these stresses set in regular patterns which is what we call METRE. A metrical unit is called a FOOT. This comes from ancient Greece, where, in dance, the foot was raised up and down on the beat of a bar of music. A metrical line is named according to the number of feet in a line.

Iambic Pentametre

Iambic has one unstressed & one stressed syllable OR one weak syllable & one strong syllable. **Iambic Pentametre** (used by Shakespeare & other writers) is made up of 5 feet of iambic rhythms.e.g. de dum/de dum/de dum/de dum/de dum. e.g. 'The clock struck nine when I did send the nurse' and 'I left no ring with her, what means this lady?' Be aware of the **hemi-stich**: where one character speaks half a line and the next character finishes the second half of the line. The rhythm of iambic pentameter resembles the beating of the human heart and is closest to natural rhythms of natural speech. Blank verse (verse without rhyme) is the closest rhythm to natural speech. It has no regular rhyme and is therefore ideal for writing verse plays. There are, however, inversions and other variations which are added to create variety in the rhythm. Shakespeare often uses prose to vary his writing too. This is often reserved for the lower status characters, but not always. It is sometimes used to depict informality.

HENRY 6TH PART 1 ACT 3 SC 3 by WILLIAM SHAKESPEARE (1591)

(Joan has persuaded the Duke of Burgundy to remain loyal to the French cause. Formerly he has sided with the English).

<u>Joan:</u>

Brave Burgundy, undoubted hope of France,
Stay. Let thy humble handmaid speak to thee.
Look on thy country, look on fertile France,
And see the cities and the towns defaced
By wasting ruin of the cruel foe.
As looks the mother on her lowly babe,
When death doth close his tender-dying eyes,
See, see the pining malady of France;
Behold the wounds, the most unnatural wounds,
Which thou thyself hast given her woeful breasts.
O turn thy edged sword another way,
Strike those that hurt, and hurt not those that help.
One drop of blood drawn from thy country's bosom
Should grieve thee more than streams of foreign gore.
Return thee, therefore, with a flood of tears,
And wash away thy country's stained spots.
Besides, all French and France exclaims on thee,
Doubting thy birth and lawful progeny.
Who join'st thou with, but with a lordly nation
That will not trust thee but for profit's sake?
When Talbot hath set foot once in France
And fashioned thee that instrument of ill,
Who then but English Henry will be lord,
And thou be thrust out like a fugitive?
Call we to mind, and mark but this for proof:
Was not the Duke of Orleans thy foe?
And was he not in England prisoner?
But when they heard he was thine enemy
They set him free, without his ransom paid,
In spite of Burgundy and all his friends.
See, then, thou fight'st against thy countrymen,

And join'st with them will be thy slaughtermen.
Come, come, return; return, thou wandering lord,
Charles and the rest will take thee in their arms.

HENRY 6TH PART 1 ACT 1 Sc 2 by WILLIAM SHAKESPEARE (1591)

(Joan of Arc tells the Dauphin of her vision to help the French army claim victory against the English. At the beginning of the scene, Reignier tries to trick Joan in to believing he is the Dauphin but Joan sees through him).

La Pucelle (Joan):

Where is the Dauphin? - Come, come from behind;
I know thee well, though never seen before.
Be not amaz'd, there is nothing hid from me:
In private will I talk with thee apart,
Stand back, you lords, and give us leave a while.

Dauphin, I am by birth a shepherd's daughter,
My wit untrain'd in any kind of art.
Heaven and our Lady gracious hath it pleas'd
To shine on my contemptible estate:
Lo! Whilst I waited on my tender lambs,
And to sun's parching heat display'd my cheeks,
God's mother deigned to appear to me;
And, in a vision full of majesty,
Will'd me to leave my base vocation,
And free my country from calamity.
Her aid she promis'd and assur'd success:
In complete glory she reveal'd herself;
And, whereas I was black and swart before,
With those clear rays, which she infus'd on me,
That beauty am I bless'd with, which you see.
Ask me what question thou canst possible,
And I will answer unpremeditated:
My courage try by combat, if thou dar'st,
And thou shalt find that I exceed my sex.
Resolve on this, - thou shalt be fortunate,
If thou receive me for thy warlike mate.

I am prepared. Here is my keen-edg'd sword,
Deck'd with five flower-de-luces on each side;

27

The which at Touraine, in Saint Katharine's churchyard,
Out of a great deal of old iron I chose forth.
(*Joan fights with Charles, to show her strength*).

Christ's mother helps me, else I were too weak.

I must not yield to any rites of love,
For my profession's sacred from above:
When I have chased all thy foes from hence,
Then will I think upon a recompense.

Assigned am I to be the English scourge.
This night the siege assuredly I'll raise:
Expect Saint Martin's summer, halcyon days,
Since I have entered into those wars.
Glory is like a circle in the water,
Which never ceaseth to enlarge itself,
Till, by broad spreading, it disperse to nought.
With Henry's death the English circle ends;
Dispersed are the glories it included.
Now am I like that proud insulting ship,
Which Caesar and his fortune bare at once.

HENRY 6th PART 3 by WILLIAM SHAKESPEARE (1591)

(Queen Margaret is furious with her weak husband, King Henry. She is determined to take charge, and to go into battle herself, if needs be. She addresses the King, whilst her son, Prince Edward, watches on).

<u>Queen Margaret:</u>

Who can be patient in such extremes?
Ah, wretched man! would I had died a maid
And never seen thee, never borne thee son,
Seeing thou hast proved so unnatural a father.
Hath he deserved to lose his birthright thus?
Had'st thou but loved him half so well as I,
Or felt that pain which I did for him once,
Or nourish'd him as I did with my blood,
Thou wouldst have left thy dearest heart-blood there,
Rather than have that savage duke thine heir
And disinherited thine only son.

Enforced thee! art thou king, and wilt be forced?
I shame to hear thee speak. Ah, timorous wretch!
Thou hast undone thyself, thy son and me;
And given unto the house of York such head
As thou shalt reign but by their sufferance.
To entail him and his heirs unto the crown,
What is it, but to make thy sepulchre
And creep into it far before thy time?
Warwick is chancellor and the lord of Calais;
Stern Falconbridge commands the narrow seas;
The duke is made protector of the realm;
And yet shalt thou be safe? such safety finds
The trembling lamb environed with wolves.
Had I been there, which am a silly woman,
The soldiers should have toss'd me on their pikes
Before I would have granted to that act.

But thou preferr'st thy life before thine honour:
And seeing thou dost, I here divorce myself
Both from thy table, Henry, and thy bed,
Until that act of parliament be repeal'd
Whereby my son is disinherited.
The northern lords that have forsworn thy colours
Will follow mine, if once they see them spread;
And spread they shall be, to thy foul disgrace
And utter ruin of the House of York.
Thus, do I leave thee. Come, son, let's away;
Our army is ready; come, we'll after them.

RICHARD 3rd ACT 1 Sc 2 by WILLIAM SHAKESPEARE (1593)

(Lady Anne is following the funeral procession of her father-in-law, Henry 6th. Half way through the scene, Richard of Gloucester appears).

Lady Anne:

Set down, set down your honorable load,
If honor may be shrouded in a hearse,
Whilst I awhile obsequiously lament
Th'untimely fall of virtuous Lancaster.

(the coffin is set down)

Poor key-cold figure of a holy king,
Pale ashes of the house of Lancaster,
Thou bloodless remnant of that royal blood:
Be it lawful that I invocate thy ghost
To hear the lamentations of poor Anne,
Wife to thy Edward, to thy slaughtered son,
Stabbed by the selfsame hand that made these wounds.
Lo, in these windows that let forth thy life,
I pour the helpless balm of my poor eyes.
O cursed be the hand that made these holes,
Cursed the blood that let this blood from hence,
Cursed the heart that had the heart to do it.
More direful hap betide that hated wretch
That makes us wretched by the death of thee
Than I can wish to wolves, to spiders, toads,
Or any creeping venomed thing that lives.
If ever he have child, abortive be it,
Prodigious, and untimely brought to light,
Whose ugly and unnatural aspect
May fright the hopeful mother at the view,
And that be heir to his unhappiness.
If ever he have wife, let her be made
More miserable by the death of him
Than I am made by my young lord and thee. –

Come now towards Chertsey with your holy load
Taken from Paul's to be interred there,

(*The Gentlemen lift the coffin*)

And still as you are weary of this weight
Rest you, whiles I lament King Henry's corpse.

(*Richard of Gloucester appears and blocks the funeral procession*)
(*The Gentlemen are afraid*)

What black magician conjures up this fiend
To stop devoted, charitable deeds?

What, do you tremble? Are you all afraid?
Alas, I blame you not, for you are mortal,
And mortal eyes cannot endure the devil. –
Avaunt, thou dreadful minister of hell.
Thou had'st but power over his mortal body;
His soul thou canst not have; therefore be gone.
(*To Richard*)
Foul devil, for God's sake hence and trouble us not,
For thou hast made the happy earth thy hell,
Filled it with cursing cries and deep exclaims.
If thou delight to view thy heinous deeds,
Behold this pattern of thy butcheries.-
O gentlemen, see, see! Dead Henry's wounds
'Ope their congealed mouths and bleed afresh! –
Blush, blush, thou lump of foul deformity,
For 'tis thy presence that ex-hales this blood
From cold and empty veins where no blood dwells.
Thy deed, inhuman and unnatural,
Provokes this deluge supernatural.
O God, which this blood mad'st, revenge his death!
O earth, which this blood drink'st, revenge his death!

RESTORATION THEATRE
1660-1666

WYCHERLEY

CONGREVE

SHERIDAN

THE RESTORATION PERIOD

The restoration period refers to the time of the restoration of the British monarchy. Charles 2nd regained the throne in 1660. Prior to this period, from 1642-1660, all theatres were closed and many had fallen into disrepair. This was during the time of the civil war when Oliver Cromwell and the parliamentarians took over Britain and all theatres were closed to prevent public disorder and were to remain closed until 1660, a total of eighteen years. The Puritans disapproved of the theatre, regarding it as immoral. The theatres were not all technically closed, some were used for other functions or gatherings.

The writing which emerged during this time was highly stylised, with overly complicated plots, stock characters and bawdiness. Most of the plays were comic in nature and style as a direct result of the harsh puritanical period which preceded it. For the first time, professional actresses emerged on the English stage. The audiences were mostly delighted at the novelty of experiencing female actors on our stages, rather than boys playing women's parts. The writing of this time was referred to as 'Restoration Comedy' or 'Comedy of Manners'. Many of the actors and actresses during this period became celebrities. There were many writers of these restoration comedies. George Etherege led the way with the comedy of intrigue and was followed by William Congreve, William Wycherley and Richard Brinsley Sheridan.

William Wycherley 1641-1716
Wycherley was best known for his plays, "The Country Wife' and 'The Plain Dealer'.

William Congreve 1670-1729
Congreve was best known for his plays, "The Old Bachelor", 'Love for Love", The Double Dealer" and "The Way of the World".

Richard Brinsley Sheridan 1751-1816
Sheridan was the owner of the Theatre Royal, Drury Lane. Sheridan was best known for his plays, "The Rivals", "The School for Scandal", "The Duenna", and "A Trip to Scarborough".

THE COUNTRY WIFE by WILLIAM WYCHERLEY
1675

(The young Margery Pinchwife is married to a jealous, older husband who tries to keep her locked away in the country, away from the attentions of men in London. On a rare trip to London, Margery has had to dress like a man, but this has not stopped the attentions of a Mr Horner. Mr Pinchwife insists his wife should write Horner a letter, scorning his advances.However, Margery is attracted to the younger Mr Horner and decides to write her own version of a letter instead).

<u>Mrs Pinchwife:</u>

'For Mr Horner' – So, I am glad he has told me his name. 'Dear Mr Horner! But why should I send thee such a letter that will vex thee, and make thee angry with me? – Well, I will not send it. – Ay, but then my husband will kill me – for I see plainly he won't let me love Mr Horner – but what care I for my husband. But oh, what if I writ at bottom my husband made me write it? Ay, but then my husband would see it. Can one have no shift?

Stay – what if I should write a letter, and wrap it up like this, and write upon't too? Ay. But then my husband would see it. I don't know what to do. – But yet evads, I'll try, so I will – for I will not send *this* letter to poor Mr Horner, come what will on't.

'Dear, sweet Mr Horner' – so – my husband would have me send you a base, rude, unmannerly letter; but I won't – so – 'and would have me to say to you, I hate you, poor Mr Horner; but I won't tell a lie for him' – there – 'for I am sure if you and I were in the country at cards together' – so – I could not help treading on your toe under the table' – so – 'or rubbing knees with you, and staring in your face, till you saw me' – very well- 'and then looking down, and blushing for an hour together' – so – but I must make haste before my husband comes: and now he has taught me to write letters, you shall have longer ones from me, who am, dear, dear, poor, dear Mr Horner, your most humble friend, and servant to command till death, - Margery Pinchwife'.

THE WAY OF THE WORLD by WILLIAM CONGREVE 1700

(Act 3, Sc 1. Foible is the young servant of Lady Wishfort, a wealthy old widow and aunt to Millamant. Foible is a witty, lively and well-liked character. She is newly and secretly wedded to Waitwell, who is Mirabell's servant. She works for Mirabell and he is very happy with the information she brings him.)

Foible:

Madam, I have seen the party.

Nay, 'tis your ladyship has done, and are to do; I have only promised. But a man so enamoured – so transported! Well, here it is, all that is left; (*Shows the picture*) all that is not kissed away. Well, if worshipping of pictures be a sin – poor Sir Rowland, I say.

So, the devil has been beforehand with me; what shall I say? (*Aside*). Alas, madam, could I help it, if I met with that confident thing? Was I at fault? If you had heard how he used me, and all upon your ladyship's account, I'm sure you would not suspect my fidelity. Nay, if that had been the worst, I could have borne; but he had a fling at your ladyship too – and then, I could not hold; but, i'faith, I gave him his own!

Oh, madam, 'tis a shame to say what he said – with his taunts and his fleers, tossing up his nose. Humh (says he), what, you are a-hatching some plot (says he), you are so early abroad, or catering (says he), ferreting, for some disbanded officer, I warrant. Half-pay is but thin subsistence (says he). Well, what pension does your lady propose? Let me see (says he), what, she must come down pretty deep now, she's superannuated (says he), and –

Poison him? Poisoning's too good for him. Starve him madam, starve him – marry Sir Rowland and get him disinherited! Oh, you would bless yourself to hear what he said.

Humh (says he), I hear you are laying designs against me too (says he), and Mrs Millamant is to marry my uncle; (he does not suspect a word of your ladyship); but (says he), I'll fit you for that I warrant you (says he), I'll hamper you for that (says he) – you and your old frippery too (says he), I'll handle you!

THE WAY OF THE WORLD by WILLIAM CONGREVE 1700

(This comic scene comes from Act 4, Sc 5. Millamant is setting out the terms and conditions necessary for her to contemplate becoming Mirabel's wife).

Millamant:

Oh, I hate a lover that can dare to think he draws a moment's air independent on the bounty of his mistress. There is not so impudent a thing in nature as the saucy look of an assured man confident of success: the pedantic arrogance of a very husband has not so pragmatical an air. Ah, I'll never marry, unless I am first made sure of my will and pleasure.

Ah, don't be impertinent. My dear liberty, shall I leave thee? My faithful solitude, my darling contemplation, must I bid you adieu? My morning thoughts, agreeable waking, indolent slumbers. I can't do it, 'tis more than impossible – positively, Mirabel, I'll lie-a-bed in the morning as long as I please.

Ah! Idle creature, get up when you will! And do you hear, I won't be called names after I'm married; I won't be called names!

Ay, as wife, spouse, my dear, joy, jewel, love, sweet-heart, and the rest of that nauseous cant in which men and their wives are so fulsomely familiar. Good Mirabel, don't let us be familiar or too fond, nor kiss before folks, like my Lady Fadler and Sir Francis; nor go to Hyde Park together the first Sunday in a new chariot, to provoke eyes and whispers. Let us never visit together, nor go to a play together, but let us be very strange and well-bred. Let us be as strange as if we had been married a great while, and as well-bred as if we were not married at all.

I want to be at liberty to pay and receive visits to and from whom I please; to write and receive letters, without interrogatories or wry faces on your part; to wear what I please, and choose conversation with regard only to my own taste; to have no obligation upon me to converse with wits that I don't like, because they are your acquaintances, or to be intimate with fools, because they may be your relations. Come to dinner when I please, dine in my dressing-room when I'm out of humour, without giving a reason. To have my closet inviolate; to be sole empress of my tea-table, which you must never presume to approach without first asking leave. And lastly, where I am, you shall always knock at the door before you come in. These articles subscribed, if I continue to endure you a little longer, I may by degrees dwindle into a wife.

THE RIVALS by R B SHERIDAN 1775

(Lydia Languish is complaining to her cousin, Julia, about the fact that everyone seems to know how she has been fooled by Beverley. She had been determined to marry a penniless soldier and now finds out that Beverley is none other than the wealthy Captain Jack Absolute).

Lydia:

Heigh-ho! Though he has used me so, this fellow runs strangely through my head. I believe one lecture from my grave cousin will make me recall him.

O Julia, I have come to you with such an appetite for consolation. – Lud! Child, what's the matter with you? You have been crying! – I'll be hanged if that Faulkland has not been tormenting you.

Ah! Whatever vexations you may have, I can assure you mine surpass them. You know who Beverley proves to be?

So, then, I see I have been deceived by every one! But I don't care – I'll never have him.

Why, is it not provoking? When I had thought we were coming to the prettiest distress imaginable, to find myself made a mere Smithfield bargain of at last! There, had I projected one of the most sentimental elopements! – so becoming a disguise! – so amiable a ladder of ropes! – Conscious moon – four horses – Scotch parson – with such surprise to Mrs Malaprop – and such paragraphs in the newspaper! – Oh, I shall die with disappointment!

Now – sad reverse! – what have I to expect, but, after a deal of flimsy preparation, with a bishops license, and my aunt's blessing, to go simpering up to the altar; or perhaps be cried three times in a country church, and have an unmannerly fat clerk ask the consent of every butcher in the parish to join John Absolute and Lydia Languish, spinster! Oh, that I should live to hear myself called spinster!

How mortifying, to remember the dear delicious shifts I used to be put to, to gain half a minute's conversation with this fellow! How often have I stole forth, on the coldest night in January, and found him in the garden, stuck like a dripping statue! There would he kneel to me in the snow, and sneeze and cough so pathetically! He shivering with cold and I with apprehension! And while the freezing blast numbed our joints, how warmly he would press me to pity his flame, and to glow with mutual ardour! – Ah, Julia, that was something like being in love.

THE SCHOOL FOR SCANDAL by RICHARD BRINSLEY SHERIDAN (1777)

(In Act 1, Sc 1, Lady Sneerwell and Verjuice enjoy a moment of plotting and scheming against their acquaintances).

Lady Sneerwell:

The paragraphs you say were all inserted:

Did you circulate the report of Lady Brittle's Intrigue with Captain Boastall?

What have you done as to the insinuation as to a certain Baronet's lady and a certain cook.

Why truly Mrs Clackit has a very pretty talent-a great deal of industry-yet-yes-has been tolerably successful in her way- to my knowledge she has been the cause of breaking off six matches, of three sons being disinherited and four daughters being turned out of doors. Of three several elopements, as many close confinements - nine separate maintenances and two divorces. But her manner is gross.

Yes, my dear Verjuice. I am no hypocrite to deny the satisfaction I reap from the success of my efforts. Wounded myself, in the early part of my life by the envenomed tongue of scandal, I confess I have since known no pleasure equal to the reducing of others to the level of my own injured reputation.

At a loss to guess your motives? I conceive you mean with respect to my neighbour, Sir Peter Teazle, and his family – And has my conduct in this matter really appeared to you so mysterious? Then, at once to unravel this mystery – I must inform you that love has no share whatsoever in the intercourse between Mr Surface and me. His real attachment is to Maria - or her fortune – but finding in his brother a favoured rival, he has been obliged to mask his pretensions – and profit by my assistance. Heavens! How dull you are! Must I confess that Charles – that libertine, that extravagant, that bankrupt in fortune and reputation

43

– that he it is for whom I am thus anxious and malicious and to gain whom I would sacrifice – everything -

How came Surface and I so confidential? For our mutual interest – but I have found out him a long time since, altho' he has contrived to deceive everybody beside – I know him to be artful selfish and malicious – while with Sir Peter and indeed with all his acquaintance, he passes for a youthful miracle of prudence – good sense and benevolence. True and with the assistance of his sentiments and hypocrisy he has brought Sir Peter entirely in his interests with respect to Maria and is now I believe attempting to flatter Lady Teazle into the same good opinion towards him – while poor Charles has no friend in the house – though I fear he has a powerful one in Maria's heart, against whom we must direct our schemes.

REALISM

CHEKHOV

IBSEN

STRINDBERG

TURGENEV

REALISM

Realism is a literary technique which describes locations, characters and themes in a realistic style without using elaborate imagery or rhetorical language. Literary realism emerged in the nineteenth century (circa 1870's) in France and was a popular modernist movement. The subjects and themes were of ordinary recognizable people, those characters readers could easily identify with. In drama, a set of theatrical conventions aim to create an illusion of reality on stage. Realism is still the dominant theatrical style today and is especially seen in film and TV.

Chekhov 1860-1904
Chekov is considered a master of realism.
His four major works are his plays: The Seagull, Uncle Vanya, The Three Sisters, and The Cherry Orchard. His play 'Ivanov' was based on an earlier play named 'The Wood Demon'. His three most popular plays, The Seagull, The Three Sisters and The Cherry Orchard were produced at Stanislavski's Moscow Arts Theatre.

Henrik Ibsen 1828-1906
Ibsen was Norwegian although he actually wrote his plays in Danish. He is a writer of realism and is often referred to as the 'father of realism'. Ibsen is known for his plays, 'Brand', 'Peer Gynt', 'An Enemy of the People', 'A Doll's House', 'Hedda Gabler,' 'Ghosts', 'The Wild Duck', 'The Master Builder'.

August Strindberg 1849-1912
Strindberg was Swedish and wrote over 60 plays.
Strindberg is known for his plays, 'Miss Julie', 'A Dream Play', 'The Father', 'The Dance of Death', 'The Stronger', 'Easter' and many more.

THE SEAGULL ACT 4 BY ANTON CHEKHOV (1896)

(The scene takes place in Sorin's House. Nina has returned and makes her peace with Konstantin Trepliov)

Nina:

Lock the doors.

How warm, how nice it is here! … Have I changed a lot?
I was afraid that you might hate me. Every night I dream that you look at me and don't recognize me. Ever since I came, I've been walking round here … beside the lake. I've been near this house many times, but I dared not come in.

Let us sit and talk …

Yesterday, late in the evening I came into the garden to see whether our stage was still there. And it is still standing! I began to cry for the first time in two years, and it lifted the weight from my heart, and I felt more at ease.

And so, you've become a writer … You are a writer and I'm an actress. I used to live here joyously, like a child – I used to wake up in the morning and burst into song. I loved you and dreamed of fame … And now? Tomorrow morning early, I have to go to Yelietz in a third-class carriage … with the peasants; and at Yelietz, upstart business men will pester me with their attentions.

Life is coarse!

I've accepted an engagement for the whole winter. It's time to go. Don't see me off, I'll go by myself.

Why did you say you kissed the ground where I walked?
I am so tired. Oh, I wish I could rest … just rest! I'm a seagull … No, that's not it. I'm an actress.

(She hears Trigorin laughing off stage) So he is here, too! …

He didn't believe in the theatre, he was always laughing at my dreams, and so gradually I ceased to believe, too, and lost heart ... And then I was so preoccupied with love and jealousy, and a constant fear for my baby ... I became petty and common, when I acted I did it stupidly ... I didn't know what to do with my hands or how to stand on the stage, I couldn't control my voice ... But you can't imagine what it feels like – when you know that you are acting abominably.

.... Do you remember you shot a seagull? A man came along by chance, saw it and destroyed it, just to pass the time ...
What was I talking about? ...Yes, about the stage. I'm not like that now ... Now I am a real actress, I act with intense enjoyment, with enthusiasm; on the stage I am intoxicated and I feel that I am beautiful. But now, while I'm living here, I go for walks a lot ... I keep walking and thinking ... thinking and feeling that I am growing stronger in spirit with every day that passes ... I think I know, that what matters in our work – whether you act on the stage or write stories – what really matters is not fame, or glamour, not the things I used to dream about – but knowing how to endure things. How to bear one's cross and have faith. I have faith now and I'm not suffering quite so much, and when I think of my vocation, I'm not afraid of life.

IVANOV ACT 3 BY ANTON CHEKHOV (1887)

(Sasha has been having an affair with the older, married, depressive Ivanov. At this point in the play, she pays a visit to his house as she has not seen him for some time and is desperate to see him. Ivanov is worried his wife may see them together).

Sasha:

I'm here! How are you? Weren't you expecting me? Why haven't you been to see us for so long?

Your wife won't see me. I came in through the back door. I'll go in a minute.

What was I to do? You haven't been to see us for a fortnight, you never answered my letters. I've been worn out with worry.

You to blame? Are you to blame because you've stopped loving your wife? A man isn't master of his feelings; you didn't want to stop loving her. Are you to blame because she saw me telling you I loved you? No, you didn't want her to see it …

You're angry with me, it was stupid of me to come here.

There are a lot of things men don't understand. Every girl is more attracted by a man who's a failure than by one who's a success, because what she wants is active love … Men are taken up with their work and so love has to take a back seat with them. To have a talk with his wife, to take a stroll with her in the garden, to pass time pleasantly with her, to weep a little on her grave – But for us – love is life. I love you, and that means that I dream about how I'd cure you of your depression, how I'd follow you to the end of the world … It would be sheer happiness for me to copy out your papers all night long, or watch over you all night so that no one woke you… I remember once you came to our house about three years ago at harvest time, and you were all covered in dust and tired out, and you asked for a drink of water. I went to get you a glass, but you were lying on the sofa, sound asleep, when I came back with it. You slept the best part of the day in our house, and I stood outside the door all the time and guarded it, so that no one should come in. And I was so happy! The greater the effort, the greater the love …

It's time I went. Good-bye! I'm afraid your honest doctor may tell your wife about my being here. Go to your wife now and stay with her … Do your duty. Experience the grief of it, ask her forgiveness, weep – that's just as it should be. But the main thing is – don't forget your work!

God bless you, Nikolai! You needn't think about me! If you write to me in about a fortnight – I'll be grateful for that. I'll write to you … Goodbye, Nikolai.

THE WILD DUCK by HENRIK IBSEN (1884)

(In Act 3, Hedvig, 14yr old daughter of Gina Ekdal and the step daughter of photographer Hjalmar Ekdal is talking to Gregers Werle. Hedvig is an innocent victim in the play. Her eyesight is failing her and she has little freedom. She is likened to the wild duck, which the family keep. The wild duck is also used as symbolism for other characters in the play. Poor Hedvig commits suicide later in the play).

Hedvig:

Good morning. Do come in, please. It's so untidy here. (*She is about to clear away the photographs).* Just a little job that I'm helping Daddy with.

Yes, the wild duck slept well last night? It looks quite different in the morning from what it does in the afternoon, and different when it's raining from when it's fine.

No, I don't go to school anymore. Because Daddy's afraid I shall hurt my eyes. He's promised to give me lessons, but he hasn't had time for it yet. In there, there are such lots of wonderful things. Yes, there are big cupboards with books in; and there are pictures in a lot of the books. And then there's an old cabinet with drawers and partitions in it; and a big clock with figures that are supposed to come out. But the clock doesn't go anymore. And then there's an old paint-box and things like that. And then all the books.

Most of the books are in English, and I don't understand that. But then I look at the pictures. There is one very large book that is called *Harryson's History of London*; that must be quite a hundred years old. And there are a tremendous lot of pictures in that. At the beginning there's a picture of Death with an hour-glass and a girl. I think that's dreadful. But then there are all the other pictures with churches and castles and streets and great ships sailing on the sea. An old sea captain lived here once and he brought them home. They called him 'The Flying Dutchman'. And that's queer, because he wasn't a Dutchman at all. In the end, he didn't come back, and left everything behind.

I want to stay at home here always and help Daddy and Mother. Not only retouching photographs. I'd like most of all to learn to engrave pictures like those in the English books. I don't think Daddy likes it. Daddy's so odd about things like that. Just think, he talks about my learning basket-weaving and straw-plaiting! But I don't see that there's anything in that. But Daddy's right in one thing. If I'd learnt to weave baskets, then I could have made the new basket for the wild duck. Because it's *my* wild duck. It belongs to me. But Daddy and Grandpapa can borrow it as often as they want to. They look after it and build things for it and that sort of thing. She is a real wild bird. And then it's so sad for her; she has no one belonging to her, poor thing. The hens have got lots of others, too, that they knew as chickens, but she's so far from all her own people, poor dear! And it's all so strange about the wild duck. There's no one who knows her. And no one who knows where she's come from, either.

THE LADY FROM THE SEA by HENRIK IBSEN (1888)

(*Ellida is talking to her husband, Wangel, about a man who she was previously romantically involved with*).

Ellida:

The day you came out to Skjoldviken and asked me to be your wife, you spoke so frankly to me about your marriage. You told me how happy you had been. I told you quite openly that I had once been in love with someone else. That we had become, in a way, engaged. It lasted such a short time. He went away. And I regarded it as finished and done with.

Do you remember, late one morning, a big American ship came into Skjoldviken for repairs? And the Captain was found dead in his cabin, he was murdered during the night. The suspect didn't drown himself. He went away in another ship, up into the Arctic. O Wangel, that is the man to whom I was engaged.

He went to sea when he was very young. And he voyaged all around the world. We talked mostly about the sea. One day he came out to look round the lighthouse. That was how we met. After that we saw each other occasionally. But this thing happened – with the captain – and he had to leave.

Early one morning – I got a note from him. In it he wrote that I was to come and meet him at Bratthammeren. I was to go out there at once, because he wanted to talk to me. Well, then he told me that he had killed the captain during the night. But he had only done what had to be done, he said. What was right. Just before he said goodbye – he took out of his pocket a key-chain, and pulled a ring off his finger, a ring he always used to wear. And he took a little ring from my finger too, and put these two rings on his keychain. Then he said that we two were going to marry ourselves to the sea. At the time it seemed – ordained. But then, thank God! He went away! I soon came to my senses, of course. I saw how mad and meaningless the whole thing had been. Yes, I heard from him. First, I got a few short lines from Archangel. He said he was going over to America. He gave me an address to reply to. I replied at once. I wrote, that everything was finished between us. And that he was not to think of me anymore, just as I would never think of him again. But, he wrote again. It was just as though I had never broken with him. He wouldn't give me up so I wrote again. I shall never be able to escape from him, the unfathomable power he has over my mind. I am afraid. Afraid of the stranger.

HEDDA GABLER by HENRIK IBSEN (1889)

(*Act 2 Hedda confides in her friend, Judge Brack on the state of her marriage to George Tesman. They have just returned from their honeymoon, but the honeymoon period appears to be over. Hedda is standing by the open French windows, loading a revolver. Judge Brack enters*).

<u>Hedda:</u>

I'm going to shoot you, Judge Brack. This'll teach you to enter houses by the back door. All right, Judge. Come along in. I was just shooting at the sky.

Well, we'll have to sit down here. And wait. Tesman won't be back for some time.

It seems ages since we had a talk. Honeymoon? Yes. Wonderful! Tesman thinks life has nothing better to offer than rooting around in libraries and copying old pieces of parchment, or whatever it is he does. But for me! Oh no, my dear Judge. I've been bored to death.

Yes. Can you imagine? Six whole months without ever meeting a single person who was one of us, and to whom I could talk about the kind of things we talk about. Having to spend every minute of one's life with the same person. As I said: every minute of one's life.

Tesman is only interested in one thing, my dear Judge. His special subject. And people who are only interested in one thing don't make the most amusing company. Not for long, anyway.

You just try it, Judge. Listening to the history of civilization morning, noon and – Oh, and those domestic industries of Brabant in the Middle Ages! That really is beyond the limit.

Why on earth did I marry George Tesman? Do you think it so very strange? I'd danced myself tired, Judge. I felt my time was up – No, I mustn't say that. Or even think it.

After all, George Tesman, he's a very respectable man. He's very clever at collecting material and all that, isn't he? I mean, he may go quite far in time. And when he came and begged me on his bended knees to be allowed to love and to cherish me, I didn't see why I shouldn't let him.

A DOLL'S HOUSE by HENRIK IBSEN (1879)

(This scene is from Act 1. Nora has helped her husband, Torvald, out of a difficult financial situation by forging her father's signature on a legal document. At this moment in the play, she is very proud of the fact that she has been able to do this and confides in her old friend, Christine Linde).

<u>Nora:</u>

He's so proud of being a man – it would be so painful and humiliating for him to know that he owed anything to me. It would completely wreck our relationship. This life we have built together would no longer exist.

I will tell him – Yes – some time, perhaps. Years from now, when I'm no longer pretty. You mustn't laugh! I mean, of course, when it no longer amuses him to see me dance and dress up and play the fool for him. Then it might be useful to have something up my sleeve.

Stupid, stupid, stupid! That time will never come. Well, what do you think of my big secret, Christine? I'm not completely useless, am I?

Mind you, all this has caused me a frightful lot of worry. It hasn't been easy for me to meet my obligations punctually. In case you don't know, in the world of business there are things called quarterly instalments and interest and they're a terrible problem to cope with. So, I've had to scrape a little here and save a little there, as best I can. I haven't been able to save much on the housekeeping money, because Torvald likes to live well; and I couldn't let the children go short of clothes – I couldn't take anything out of what he gives me for them. The poor little angels!

Whenever Torvald gave me money to buy myself new clothes, I never used more than half of it; and I always bought what was cheapest and plainest. Thank heaven anything suits me, so that Torvald's never noticed. But it made me a bit sad sometimes, because it's lovely to wear pretty clothes. Don't you think? And then I've found one or two other sources of income. Last winter I managed to get a lot of copying to do. So, I shut myself away and wrote every evening, late into the night. Oh, I often got so tired, so tired. But it was great fun, though, sitting there working and earning money. It was almost like being a man.

How much have I managed to pay off like this? Well, I can't say exactly. It's awfully difficult to keep an exact check on these kind of transactions. I only know I've paid everything I've managed to scrape together. Sometimes I really didn't know where to turn. Then I'd sit here and imagine some rich old gentleman had fallen in love with me … and that he died, and when they opened his will it said in big letters: 'Everything I possess is to be paid forthwith to my beloved Mrs Nora Helmer, in cash'.

Great heavens, there wasn't any old gentleman; he was just something I used to dream up as I sat here evening after evening wondering how on earth I could raise some money. But what does it matter? The old bore can stay imaginary as far as I'm concerned, because now I don't have to worry any longer!

Oh, Christine, isn't it wonderful? I don't have to worry anymore! No more troubles! I can play all day with the children, I can fill the house with pretty things, just the way Torvald likes. And, Christine, it'll soon be spring, and the air will be fresh and the skies blue – and then perhaps we'll be able to take a little trip somewhere. I shall be able to see the sea again. Oh, yes, yes, it's a wonderful thing to be alive and happy!

A DOLL'S HOUSE by HENRIK IBSEN (1879)

(This scene comes from Act 3. Nora has finally decided that she must leave her husband, Torvald. She has been treated like a doll-wife for far too long and after Torvald reacts badly to her actions which were intended only to help him. She now feels she can no longer stay with him).

Nora:

You and I have much to say to one another. I have a lot to talk over with you.

You don't understand me, and I have never understood you either – before tonight. No, you mustn't interrupt me. You must simply listen to what I say. Torvald, this is a settling of accounts.

Does it not occur to you that this is the first time we two, you and I, husband and wife, have had a serious conservation?

In all these eight years – longer than that – from the very beginning of our acquaintance we have never exchanged a word on any serious subject.

I have been greatly wronged, Torvald – first by Papa and then by you.

You have never loved me. You have only thought it pleasant to be in love with me.

When I was at home with Papa, he told me his opinion about everything, and so I had the same opinions; and if I differed from him, I concealed the fact, because he would not have liked it. He called me his doll child, and he played with me just as I used to play with my dolls. And when I came to live with you – I was simply transferred from Papa's hands to yours. You arranged everything according to your own taste. I have existed merely to perform tricks for you, Torvald. You and Papa have committed a great sin against me. It is your fault that I have made nothing of my life.

Our home has been nothing but a playroom. I have been your doll wife, just as at home I was Papa's doll child; and here the children have been my dolls. That is what our marriage has been, Torvald.

Torvald, you are not the man to educate me into being a proper wife for you. I must try and educate myself. And that is why I am going to leave you now. I must stand quite alone if I am to understand myself and everything about me. I will take with me what belongs to myself. I will take nothing from you, either now or later. Tomorrow I shall go home – I mean to my old home. It will be easiest for me to find something to do there. I believe that before all else I am a reasonable human being just as you are – and I must try and become one. Torvald, most people would think you right and that views of that kind are to be found in books; but I can no longer content myself with what most people say. I have never felt my mind so clear and certain as tonight.

I have heard that when a wife deserts her husband's house, as I am doing now, he is legally freed from all obligations toward her. You are not to feel yourself bound in the slightest way, any more than I shall. There must be perfect freedom on both sides. See, here is your ring back. Give me mine. Now it is all over.

MISS JULIE by AUGUST STRINDBERG (1888)

(On a country estate in Sweden. Midsummer's Eve. The kitchen. Miss Julie is 25yrs old and the daughter of a Count. She has been brought up to hate men and since her engagement to a lawyer was broken off, she hates them even more. In this scene, she is talking to Jean, her father's valet).

Miss Julie:

We must run away! But first we must talk – that is, I must talk – so far, you've been doing all the talking. You've told me about your life, now I must tell you about myself, so that we know all about each other before we go away together.

My mother was a commoner, of quite humble birth. She was brought up with ideas about equality, freedom for women and all that. And she had a decided aversion to marriage. So, when my father proposed to her, she replied that she would never become his wife, but that he could become her lover. My father told her that he had no desire to see the woman he loved enjoy less respect than himself. When she explained that the world's respect did not concern her, he agreed to her conditions. But now he was cut off from his social circle and confined to his domestic life, which could not satisfy him. And then? I came into the world, against my mother's wish as far as I can gather. She wanted to bring me up as a child of nature, and into the bargain I was to learn everything that a boy has to learn so that I might stand as an example of how a woman can be as good as a man. I had to wear boy's clothes, and learn to look after horses – though I was never allowed to enter the cowshed. I had to groom and saddle them, and hunt – even learn to slaughter animals. That was horrible. Meanwhile, on the estate, all the men were set to perform the women's tasks, and the women the men's – so that it began to fail, and we became the laughing-stock of the district. In the end my father put his foot down, and everything was changed back to the way he wanted it. That was when they married. Then my mother fell ill – what illness, I don't know – but she often had convulsions, hid herself, in the attic and the garden, and sometimes stayed out all night. Then there was the great fire which you have heard about. The house, the stables and the cowshed were all burned down, under circumstances suggesting arson – for the accident happened the very day our quarterly insurance had expired, and the premium my father sent had been delayed through the inefficiency of the servant carrying it, so that it hadn't arrived in time.(*She fills her glass and drinks*). So, we were left penniless, and had to sleep in the carriages. My father couldn't think where he would be able to find the money to rebuild the house, as he'd cut himself off from his old friends. Then mother advised him to ask for a loan from an old friend of hers, a brick merchant who lived in the neighbourhood. Father got the money, free of interest, which rather surprised him. So, the house was rebuilt. Do you know who burned the house down? My mother! Do you know who the brick merchant was? My mother's lover! Do you know whose the money was? It was my mother's.

My mother had little money of her own, which she didn't want my father to have control of. So, she entrusted it to her – friend.

Exactly. He kept it. All this came to my father's knowledge – but he couldn't start an action, repay his wife's lover, or prove that the money was his wife's. It was my mother's revenge on him, for taking control of the house out of her hands. He was on the verge of shooting himself – the rumour was that he had done so, but had failed to kill himself. Well, he lived; and he made my mother pay for what she had done. Those five years were dreadful for me, I can tell you. I was sorry for my father, but I took my mother's side, because I didn't know the circumstances. I'd learned from her to distrust and hate men – she hated men. And I swore to her that I would never be a slave to any man.

A MONTH IN THE COUNTRY by IVAN TURGENEV (1855)

(Natalia Petrovna has asked to see Vera in order to probe her about her feelings for the new tutor, Alexei Nikolaich. Both women have feelings for him but the older, more sophisticated Natalia, dominates and manipulates the conversation).

Natalia Petrovna:

Ah, Verochka!

Vera, I want to have a little talk with you. A serious talk. Sit down my dear, will you? *(Vera sits)* Now…. Vera, one thinks of you as still a child; but it's high time you gave a thought to your future. You're an orphan and not a rich one at that: sooner or later you are bound to tire of living on somebody else's property. Now how would you like suddenly to have control or your very own house?

You are being sought in marriage. *(Vera stares at her, a pause)* You didn't expect this? I must confess I didn't either, you are still so young. I refuse to press you in the slightest- but I thought it my duty to let you know. *(As Vera suddenly covers her face with her hands)* Vera! My dear… what is it? But you're shaking like a leaf!

In my power? Vera, what do you take me for? In my power indeed- will you please take that back this minute? I command you! *(Vera smiles)* That's better… Vera my child, I tell you what- you make believe I'm your elder sister. Now one fine day your sister comes to you and says, "what do you think, little one? Somebody is asking for your hand!" well what would be your first thought?

You're too young? Good; your sister would agree, the suitor would be given no for an answer, fini! But suppose he was a very nice gentlemen with means, prepared to bide his time, … what then? Ah, you're curious. Can't you guess? ……. Bolshinstov. It's true he's not very young, and not wildly prepossessing… He's on the right side of fifty! Well, Bolshinstov, my dear, you are dead and buried, may you rest in peace… It was foolish of me to forget that little girl's dream of marrying for love.

Didn't I marry for love? Yes, of course I did … eh bien fini! Bolshinstov, you are dismissed… There! And you're not frightened of me anymore? Well then, Verochka darling, just whisper quietly into my ear… you don't want to marry Bolshinstov because he's too old- but is that the only reason?

I realize you can never fall in love with Bolshinstov; but he's an excellent man. And if there is nobody else…. Isn't there anybody you're fond of?

Vera you must know what I mean… Out of the Young men you've met… have you formed any attachment at all?

What about our philosopher Rakitin? An elder brother, I see… And the new tutor?

Alexei Nikoliach? He is nice, isn't he? Such a pity he's so bashful with everybody -..

Isn't he?

Afraid of me? How do you know? He told you… I never knew you two were such good friends. You must be careful Vera. I know he's a very pleasant young man, but at your age, it's not quite, people might think - but as you like him, and nothing more, then there is no real need for me to say another word. Is there?

Vera is that the way you look at a sister? Those eyes are dying to tell me something…

My poor Vera…My poor sweet, and he… what of him?
You imagine what? That you see a look in his eyes… as if he thought of you as a special person …

No there's nothing the matter. Not in the least, I just want to be by myself.

THE VICTORIANS

THOMAS HARDY

OSCAR WILDE

GEORGE BERNARD SHAW

CHARLES DICKENS

THOMAS HARDY 1840-1928
ENGLISH NOVELIST & POET

Thomas Hardy is known for his lengthy, detailed novels almost all of which have been turned into films or TV drama. He also writes in the style of realism. His pessimistic view on life often results in his protagonist's unhappiness. The power of nature and man's destiny is also evident in his writing. His novels include: Tess of the d'Urbervilles, Far from the Madding Crowd, Jude the Obscure, The Mayor Casterbridge & The Return of the Native.

TESS OF THE D'URBERVILLES by THOMAS HARDY (1892)

(19th Century Wessex. Angel has returned from Brazil to tell Tess he has forgiven her. Tess tells Angel that she is still living with Alec D'Urberville. Shortly after, she stabs Alec D'Urberville to death. In this scene, she is telling Angel what she has done and he helps Tess to escape. The couple finally reach Stonehenge where they are later discovered by the police. Tess is eventually executed for the murder of Alec D'Urberville).

Tess:

I have done it. I have killed him, I don't know how. Still, I owed it to you, and to myself, Angel. I feared long ago, when I struck him on the mouth with my glove, that I might do it someday. He trapped me when I was too young to know better. He has wronged me – and you, Angel, through me. He has come between us and ruined us. He can't do that anymore. I never loved him as I love you. You do know that, don't you? You left me and didn't come back. What was I to do? I had to go back to him. Why did you leave me? Don't you know how much I love you? I don't blame you, but … I killed him so that you might forgive my sin against you. You will forgive me, won't you, now I have proved my love? It came to me like a shining light that this was the way I could get you back. I can't bear to be without you – you've no idea how entirely I was unable to bear you not loving me. Say you love me, Angel. Say you love me.

He heard me crying about you and he said terrible things to me. He called you a foul name and then I did it. I could not bear it. He had nagged me about you before. Then I dressed myself and came away to find you. You do love me, don't you, Angel? You do forgive me?

FAR FROM THE MADDING CROWD by THOMAS HARDY (1874)

(Bathsheba meets local sheep farmer, Gabriel Oak. Gabriel gives Bathsheba an ailing lamb and then proposes to her).

Bathsheba:

Bathsheba Everdene. Bathsheba. The name has always sounded strange to me. I don't like to hear it said out loud. My parents died when I was very young, so there was no one to ask where it came from. I've grown accustomed to being on my own. Some say, even too accustomed. Too independent.
(*Gabriel returns a scarf she has lost).*
My scarf! I lost it. Thankyou. You must be Farmer Oak.
My aunt has told me about you. I'm working on her farm for the winter. This is your land. I'm trespassing.

Good afternoon, Farmer Oak. (*She wanders amongst the sheep).*

What is this one called? (referring to one of Gabriel's sheep)

Old George… (*some moments of awkward silence).*

Marry me?

No… I should hope not.

No, there is no one waiting for me?

No, but that doesn't mean I'll marry you!

Mr Oak! Mr Oak, wait! I didn't say I wouldn't marry you, either! I haven't really thought about it.

You're better off than I, Mr Oak. I have an education and nothing more. You could do much, much better than me.

You'd grow to despise me. Mr Oak, I don't want a husband. I'd hate to be some man's property. I shouldn't mind being a bride at a wedding if I could be one without getting a husband. I'm too independent for you. If I ever were to marry, I'd want somebody to tame me and you'd never be able to do it. You'd grow to despise me.

ON THE WESTERN CIRCUIT by THOMAS HARDY (1894)

(Edith is helping her servant girl, Anna, to write a letter to a man she has recently met at a Fair. During the time she has been helping Anna to write these letters of affection, she has begun to develop feelings for the recipient himself. This is largely due to the fact that she is in a loveless marriage).

Edith:

Anna, this is NOT good enough. It really isn't. I can't believe you're even trying.

But with the copy staring you in the face surely it's not too much to ask you to SPELL the words correctly. Look – you've left the 'e' out of Charles all the way down the page.

The fact is you're not putting your mind to it. And you must. I'd have thought, for the sake of someone you say you love, you'd have been only too anxious to work hard at your writing. What kind of a wife are you going to be, Anna?

But you're NOT married, Anna – not yet. There are nearly four more weeks until the wedding-day, and that means at least seven or eight MORE letters have still to be written. WHO is going to write them?

At least you could have written the letters yourself. As it is – there's only one thing I can do. He must be told, of course. He must be told that all this time, I've been answering his letters for you. Because, once you're married, he's bound to find out – Anna! Can't you see that a marriage built on a deceit – could so easily become the most bitter and loveless existence imaginable?

There are other things to consider, Anna. It was the letters and only the letters that made him decide to marry you. MY letters, Anna.

Oh yes, he loves you in a physical sense. But to give his sudden passion some lasting value, he was looking for something more. Well, he found it – in my letters. He told me. So now you see, don't you, how terribly wicked it would be not to tell him the truth?

Why, apart from wanting to know when he was coming again, you've never shown the slightest interest in his letters, either. Each letter from him has marked a step forward to which I always had to respond. So, it's not you he's come to know, Anna, but me.

I don't care, Anna. And it's not only him I'm thinking of – I'm thinking of the effect it's having on me.

Oh, you poor, stupid little fool! Can't you see what it's meant to me to have had to write to this man in terms which are now virtually those of a wife? To have had to lay bare my deepest, most intimate feelings and then – pretend to a physical condition which isn't mine at all? Every letter I wrote was written from my heart and nobody else's. And I won him, Anna. I won him.

Do you think a man like him would have let himself be captured by a common, ignorant servant girl? Those were MY thoughts and MY feelings he responded to, and for the first time in my life I feel I'm no longer alone. I've someone to love and care about –

CHARLES DICKENS
ENGLISH NOVELIST
1812-1870

Perhaps the greatest novelist of the Victorian era. His writing style is distinctive and extremely detailed, full of satire and humour. His characters are colourful, well-loved and well-known. His most famous novels are: Oliver Twist, A Christmas Carol, Nicholas Nickleby, David Copperfield, A Tale of Two Cities, Hard Times, Heartbreak House and Great Expectations.

THE OLD CURIOSITY SHOP by CHARLES DICKENS (1840)

(14 yr old Nell is an orphan. She is a very sweet and honest girl. Nell lives with her grandfather in his antique shop called 'The Old Curiosity Shop'. Nell is talking to Mrs Quilp about her grandfather who has recently mysteriously been absent from home at night due to turning to gambling in an effort to make money for his family. He eventually loses his shop and he and Nell are turned out into the streets. Nell dies at the end of the story).

Nell:

I used to read to him by the fireside, and he sat listening and when I stopped and we began to talk, he told me about my mother and how she once looked and spoke just like me when she was a little child. Then he used to take me on his knee and try to make me understand that she was not lying in her grave, but had flown to a beautiful country beyond the sky where nothing ever died or grew old – we were very happy once. I cry very seldom – but I have kept this to myself for a long time and I am not quite well, I think, for the tears come into my eyes and I cannot keep them back. I don't mind telling you my grief, for I know you will not tell it to any one again. We often walked in the field and among the green trees, and when we came home at night, we liked it better for being tired and said what a happy place it was. And if it was dark and rather dull, we used to say, what did it matter to us, for it only made us remember our last walk with greater pleasure and look forward to our next one. But now we never have those walks and though it is the same house it is darker and much more gloomy, than it used to be, indeed.

Mind you, don't suppose that grandfather is less kind to me than he was. I think he loves me better every day and is kinder and more affectionate than he was the day before. You do not know how fond he is of me. I am sure he loves me dearly, as dearly as I love him. But I have not told you the greatest change of all, and this you must never breathe again to anyone. He has no sleep or rest but that which he takes by day in his easy chair; for every night, and almost all night long, he is away from home. When he comes home in the morning, which is generally just before day, I let him in. Last night he was very late and it was quite light. I saw that his face was deadly pale, that his eyes were bloodshot, and that his legs trembled as he walked. When I had gone to bed again, I heard him groan. I got up and ran back to him and heard him say, before he knew that I was there, that he could not bear his life much longer and if it were not for the child, would wish to die. What shall I do?

THE OLD CURIOSITY SHOP by CHARLES DICKENS (1840)

(14 yr old Nell is an orphan. She is a very sweet and honest girl. Nell lives with her grandfather in his antique shop called 'The Old Curiosity Shop'. Nell is talking to her grandfather. He has recently mysteriously been absent from home at night due to turning to gambling in an effort to make money for his family. He eventually loses his shop and he and Nell are turned out into the streets. Nell optimistically suggests they leave and beg for a living. Unfortunately, Nell dies at the end of the story).

Nell:

Mr Quilp told me exactly what I told you, dear grandfather, indeed. Nothing more. What if we are beggars? Let us be beggars, and be happy. Dear Grandfather, I am not a child in that I think, but even, even if I am, oh hear me pray that we may beg, or work in open roads or fields, to earn a scanty living, rather than live as we do now. Yes, yes, rather than live as we do now. If you are sorrowful, let me know why and be sorrowful too; if you waste away and are paler and weaker every day, let me be your nurse and try to comfort you. If you are poor, let us be poor together, but let me be with you, do let me be with you, do not let me see such change and not know why, or I shall break my heart and die. Dear Grandfather, let us leave this sad place tomorrow, and beg our way from door to door.

Let us be beggars. I have no fear but we shall have enough, I am sure we shall. Let us walk through country places, and sleep in fields and under trees, and never think of money again, or anything than can make you sad, but rest at nights, and have the sun and wind upon our faces in the day, and thank God together. Let us never set foot in dark rooms or melancholy houses anymore, but wander up and down wherever we like to go, and when you are tired, you shall stop to rest in the pleasantest place that we can find, and I will go and beg for us both.

HARD TIMES by CHARLES DICKENS (1854)

(Thomas Gradgrind is a wealthy merchant who now runs a school in Coketown. Sissy Jupe used to work for a travelling circus with her father. She now lives, studies and works at the Gradgrind's school. In this scene she is telling Louisa Gradgrind about her previous life in the travelling circus).

Sissy Jupe:

Mother died when I was born. She was a dancer. Father and I travelled about the country and had no fixed place to live in. Father's a … a clown. Yes, but sometimes the people wouldn't laugh and then Father cried, he was far, far timider than they thought.

Father said I was his comfort through everything? I hope so and Father said I was. I used to read to him to cheer his courage and he was very fond of that. Oftener and oftener the stories made him forget all his troubles. O, he liked the books very much!

Father was always kind. To the last. Always, always! Kinder and kinder than I can tell, he was angry only one night, but that was not to me but to Merrylegs. Merrylegs was his performing dog. Father told Merrylegs to jump onto the backs of two chairs and stand across them, which was one of his tricks. He looked at Father and didn't do it at once, so he beat the dog and I was frightened and cried "Father, Father stop! Father pray don't hurt the creature who is so fond of you! Father stop!" And he stopped, and the dog was bloody and he lay down crying on the floor with the dog in his arms, and the dog licked his face." This is how it ended Miss Louisa. One day, after I came home from school, I found father rocking himself by the fire as though he was in pain. The more I spoke to him, the more he said nothing but, "my darling" and "my love"! he sent me to get some medicine for him and when I came back – he was gone! But I know he will come back one day. I keep the nine oils waiting for him.

GREAT EXPECTATIONS by CHARLES DICKENS (1860)

(This scene is taken from the final chapter of the novel. Estella and Pip meet once again, for the final time. The bond is as strong as ever, and yet still, they part).

Estella:

Pip, I am greatly changed. I wonder you know me.

I have never been here since. I have very often hoped and intended to come back, but have been prevented by many circumstances. Poor, poor old place!

Were you wondering, as you walked along, how it came to be left in this condition? The ground belongs to me. It is the only possession I have not relinquished. Everything else has gone from me, little by little, but I have kept this. It was the subject of the only determined resistance I made in all the wretched years.

It is to be built on. At last it is. I came here to take leave of it before its change. And you, you live abroad still? And do well, I am sure?

I have often thought of you, of late, very often. There was a long hard time when I kept far from me the remembrance of what I had thrown away when I was quite ignorant of its worth. But, since my duty has not been incompatible with the admission of that remembrance, I have given it a place in my heart.

I little thought, that I should take leave of you in taking leave of this spot. I am very glad to do so. God bless you! God forgive you! And if you could say that to me then, you will not hesitate to say that to me now – now, when suffering has been stronger than all other teaching, and has taught me to understand what your heart used to be. I have been bent and broken, but – I hope – into a better shape. Be as considerate and good to me as you were, and tell me we are friends. And we will continue friends apart.

GREAT EXPECTATIONS by CHARLES DICKENS (1860)

(Pip meets with Estella. Pip is still in love with her and tells her so. She informs him that she is to marry Bentley Drummle).

Estella:

It seems that there are sentiments, fancies – I don't know how to call them – which I am not able to comprehend. When you say you love me, I know what you mean, as a form of words; but nothing more. You address nothing in my breast, you touch nothing there. I don't care for what you say at all. I have tried to warn you of this; now, have I not? Yes. But you would not be warned, for you thought I did not mean it. Now, did you not think so?

It is in my nature. It is in the nature formed within me. I make a great difference between you and all other people when I say so much. I can do no more. It is quite true. Bentley Drummle is in town here, and pursuing me.

Why not tell you the truth, I am going to be married to him. The preparations for my marriage are making, and I shall be married soon. Why do you injuriously introduce the name of my mother by adoption? It is my own act.

On whom should I fling myself away upon the man that I took nothing to him? There! It is done. I shall do well enough, and so will my husband. As to leading me into what you call this fatal step, Miss Havisham would have had me wait, and not marry yet; but I am tired of the life I have led, which has very few charms for me, and I am willing enough to change it. Say no more. We shall never understand each other. Don't be afraid of my being a blessing to him, I shall not be that. Come! Here is my hand. Do we part on this, you visionary boy – or man?

Nonsense, this will pass in no time. You will get me out of your thoughts in a week.

GREAT EXPECTATIONS by CHARLES DICKENS (1860)

(From the Chapter in the novel, 'Miss Havisham's Remorse'. Miss Havisham attempts to make peace with Pip).

<u>Miss Havisham:</u>

'Tis noble of you to tell me that you have other causes of unhappiness. Is it true?

Can I only serve you, Pip, by serving your friend? Regarding that as done, is there nothing I can do for you yourself?

You are still on friendly terms with Mr Jaggers? This is an authority to him to pay you that money, to lay out at your irresponsible discretion for your friend. I keep no money here; but if you would rather Mr Jaggers knew nothing of the matter, I will send it to you. *(Miss Havisham writes a note to explain that she is giving Pip money and he is clear from any suspicion of profiting by the receipt of the money).* My name is on the first leaf. If you can ever write under my name, 'I forgive her,' though ever so long after my broken heart is dust – pray do it!'.

O! What have I done!, What have I done! *(referring to her interference in the relationship between Estella and Pip)*. What have I done! What have I done! Until you spoke to her the other day, and until I saw in you a looking-glass that showed me what I once felt myself, I did not know what I had done. What have I done! But Pip – my dear! Believe this: when she first came to me, I meant to save her from misery like my own. At first, I meant no more. But, as she grew, and promised to be very beautiful, I gradually did worse, and with my praises, and with my jewels, and with my teachings, and with this figure of myself always before her, a warning to back and point my lessons, I stole her heart away and put ice in its place. If you knew all my story, you would have some compassion for me and a better understanding of me. I don't know whose child was Estella! But Mr Jaggers brought her here, or sent her here? I had been shut up in these rooms a long time (I don't know how long; you know what time the clocks keep here), when I told him that I wanted a little girl to rear and love, and save from my fate. I had first seen him when I sent for him to lay this place waste for me; having read of him in the newspapers before I and the world parted. He told me that he would look about him for such an orphan child. One night he brought her here asleep, and I called her Estella. She was two or three. She herself knows nothing, but that she was left an orphan and I adopted her.

What have I done! When she first came, I meant to save her from misery like mine.

Take the pencil and write under my name, 'I forgive her!'.

OSCAR WILDE

IRISH DRAMATIST
1854-1900

OSCAR WILDE

Oscar Wilde's writing style is unique. He writes with a mixture of realism and fantasy. His observation of character and social status puts him among the best of writers. His wit, intellect and use of satire is highly amusing, decadent and extremely critical. His plays are considered 'comedy of manners' and provide a satirical portrayal of behaviour amongst the upper echelons of Victorian society. His portrayal of wealth, snobbery and morality are insurmountable. He satirises the repression of the upper classes of Victorian Britain and examines the morality and philosophy of the period. His use of language is superb and his dialogue realistic. Oscar Wilde is by far one of the most influential writers of the nineteenth century.

AESTHETICISM

Oscar Wilde was a member of the aesthetic movement; a method used to promote or educate readers about important artistic expression in society. Aestheticism originated in France from Theophile Gautier. Oscar Wilde is considered the father of aesthetics in Britain. Other writers from this movement are: Algernon Charles Swinborne, Dante Gabriel Rossetti, William Morris, John Ruskin, Max Beerbohm and John Keats. The movement started during the 1860's by a group of artists, writers, and designers. They believed that literature should study beauty in its natural form. There should be an appreciation of the beauty of the writing or literature. Gautier (1811-1872) quoted "l'art pour l'art"; art for arts' sake. Writing should create a lasting, beautiful image and does not need to be political or didactic. It should be purely for the literary experience. It should be in the present, spontaneous, and in this respect, is considered hedonistic. In many ways, this style of writing emerged in retaliation against the oppression and puritanical aspect of Victorian society. Wilde certainly liked to cause a stir and pursued a hedonistic lifestyle. The movement believed good writing should affect the way we feel and should enhance our individual natural beauty. The reader should learn from the writing, whilst at the same time, appreciate the literary aspects of the writing: the use of grammar, rhythm, rhetoric and vocabulary. The components or aesthetic writing are: aesthetic fascination, aesthetic appraisal, aesthetic emotion and aesthetic perception.

Literature is crucial to our lives because it connects us to universal truths and ideas. Through literature, writers record their thoughts, feelings, experiences and share it with others through a fictional world.

Oscar Wilde considered that art was the only worthy element of life and the only thing worth living for. He lived his life in pursuit of beauty.

The association of Aestheticism also had an effect on costume and dress. There was a rejection of tightly laced corsets and a leaning towards natural fabrics. Oscar Wilde deplored Parisian couture, preferring natural, yet beautiful clothing. It is evident from his plays that he satirizes the manners and the restrictive, highly formalised costumes of the Victoria period.

PLAYING WILDE

It is essential to adopt the correct style of speaking when playing Wilde. Clipped, crisp diction and rounded vowel sounds are essential for this period. An awareness of the style of costume should also be considered. It is necessary to adopt the correct posture and elegance of the period. Knowledge of the use of the fan might be useful for playing some scenes.

THE PICTURE OF DORIAN GRAY by OSCAR WILDE (1890)

(Dorian Gray has fallen in love with the actress, Sibyl Vane. Sibyl now realizes that her acting career fades in comparison with her love for Dorian).

Sibyl Vane:

Dorian, Dorian, before I knew you, acting was the one reality of my life. It was for only theatre that I lived. I thought that it was all true. I was Rosalind one night, and Portia the other. The joy of Beatrice was my joy, and the sorrows of Cordelia were mine also. I believed in everything. The common people who acted with me seemed to me to be godlike. The painted scenes were my world. I knew nothing but shadows, and I thought them real. You came – oh, my beautiful love! – and you freed my soul from prison. You taught me what reality really is. Tonight, for the first time in my life, I saw through the hollowness, the sham, the silliness of the empty pageant in which I had always played. Tonight, for the first time, I became conscious that the Romeo was hideous, and old, and painted, that the moonlight in the orchard was false, that the scenery was vulgar, and that the words I had to speak were unreal, were not my words, were not what I wanted to say. You had brought me something higher, something of which all art is but a reflection. You had made me understand what love really is. My love! Prince Charming! I have grown sick of shadows. You are more to me than all art can ever be. What have I to do with the puppets of a play? When I came tonight, I could not understand how it was that everything had gone from me. I thought that I was going to be wonderful. I found that I could do nothing. Suddenly it dawned on my soul what it all meant. The knowledge was exquisite to me. I heard them hissing, and I smiled. What could they know of love such as ours? Take me away, Dorian – take me away with you, where we can be quite alone. I hate the stage. I might mimic a passion that I do not feel, but I cannot mimic one that burns me like fire. Oh, Dorian, Dorian, you understand now what is signifies? Even if I could do it, it would be profanation for me to play at being in love. You have made me see that that.

THE IMPORTANCE OF BEING EARNEST ACT 2
by OSCAR WILDE (1895)

(Cecily and Algernon are alone in the garden. Cecily, much to Algernon's astonishment, tells him they are already engaged and have been so for the past three months).

Cecily Cardew:

I don't think that you should tell me you love me wildly, passionately, devotedly, hopelessly. Hopelessly doesn't make much sense, does it? Uncle Jack would be very much annoyed if he knew you were staying on till next week at the same hour.

You silly boy! Why, we have been engaged for the last three months. It will be exactly three months on Thursday.

Well, ever since dear Uncle Jack first confessed to us that he had a younger brother who was very wicked and bad, you, of course, have formed the chief topic of conversation between myself and Miss Prism. And of course, a man who is very much talked about is always very attractive. One feels there must be something in him after all. I daresay, it was foolish of me, but I fell in love with you, Ernest. On the 14th of February last. Worn out by your entire ignorance of my existence, I determined to end the matter one way or the other, and after a long struggle with myself I accepted you under this dear old tree here. The next day, I brought this little ring in your name, and this bangle with a true lover's knot, which I promised you always to wear. You have wonderfully good taste, Ernest. It's the excuse I've always given you for leading such a bad life.

And this is the box in which I keep all your dear letters. I remember only too well that I was forced to write your letters for you. I always wrote three times a week and sometimes oftener. I couldn't possibly let you read them: they would make you far too conceited. The three you wrote me after we had broken off the engagement are so beautiful, and yet so badly spelled, that even now I can hardly read them without just crying a little.

Our engagement was broken off on the 22nd of March, you can see the entry if you like. "Today broke of engagement with Ernest. Feel it is better to do so. The weather still continues to be charming". It would hardly have been a really serious engagement if it hadn't been broken off at least once. But I forgave you before the week was out. You dear, romantic boy. I don't think that I could break it off now that I have actually met you. Besides, there is of course, the question of your name. You must not laugh at me, darling, but it had always been a girlish dream of mine to love someone whose name was Ernest. There is something in that name that seems to inspire absolute confidence. I pity any poor married woman whose husband is not called Ernest. But I don't like the name of Algernon. I might respect you, Ernest, I might admire your character, but I fear that I should not be able to give you my undivided attention.

AN IDEAL HUSBAND ACT 2 BY OSCAR WILDE (1895)

(Mabel Chiltern, is Sir Robert Chiltern sister. She is a lively young girl who is very popular. In this scene, she is visiting her sister in law, Gertrude. She is complaining of the fact that her brother's secretary, Tommy Trafford, is paying her too much attention).

Mabel Chiltern:

Tommy Trafford is in great disgrace.

Gertrude, I wish you would speak to Tommy Trafford.

Well, Tommy has proposed to me again. Tommy really does nothing but propose to me. He proposed to me last night in the music-room, when I was quite unprotected, as there was an elaborate trio going on. I didn't dare to make the smallest repartee, I need hardly tell you. If I had, it would have stopped the music at once. Musical People are so absurdly unreasonable. They always want one to be perfectly dumb at the very moment when one is longing to be absolutely deaf. Then he proposed to me in broad daylight this morning, in front of that dreadful statue of Achilles. Really, the things that go on in front of that work of art are quite appalling. The police should interfere. At luncheon I saw by the glare in his eye that he was going to propose again, and I just managed to check him in time by assuring him that I was a bimetallist. Fortunately, I don't know what bimetallism means. And I don't believe anybody else does either. But the observation crushed Tommy for ten minutes. He looked quite shocked. And then Tommy is so annoying in the way he proposes. If he proposed at the top of his voice, I would not mind so much. That might produce some effect on the public. But he does it in a horrid, confidential way. When Tommy wants to be romantic, he talks to one just like a doctor. I am very fond of Tommy, but his methods of proposing are quite out of date. I wish, Gertrude, you would speak to him, and tell him that once a week is quite often enough to propose to anyone, and that it should always be done in a manner that attracts some attention.

I know, dear. You married a man with a future, didn't you? But then, Robert was a genius, and you have a noble, self-sacrificing character. You can stand geniuses. I have no character at all, and Robert is the only genius I could ever bear. As a rule, I think they are quite impossible. Geniuses talk so much don't they? Such a bad habit! And they are always thinking about themselves when I want them to be thinking about me. I must go around now and rehearse at Lady Basildon's. You remember we are having tableau, don't you? The Triumph of something, I don't know what! I hope it will be the triumph of me. Only triumph I am really interested in at present.

Oh, Gertrude, do you know who is coming to see you? That dreadful Mrs Cheveley in a most lovely gown! I assure you she is coming upstairs, as large as life and not nearly so natural.

GEORGE BERNARD SHAW
IRISH DRAMATIST
1856-1950

Shaw wrote over 60 plays. He was a comedic writer as well as a socialist and addressed issues such as poverty, capitalism and women's rights. He wished to transform society through education. His most well-known plays are: Pygmalion, Arms & The Man, Mrs Warren's Profession, Candida, Major Barbara, Heartbreak House, Androcles & the Lion, You Never Can Tell & Back to Methuselah.

ARMS AND THE MAN BY GEORGE BERNARD SHAW (1894)

(Raina is engaged to a soldier named Sergius. Raina romanticizes love and war. The play takes place during the Serbo-Bulgarian War).

Raina:

I am so happy, so proud. It proves that all our ideas were real after all. Our ideas of what Sergius would do. Our patriotism. Our heroic ideals. I sometimes used to doubt whether they were anything but dreams. Oh, what faithless little creatures' girls are. When I buckled on Sergius's sword, he looked so noble: it was treason to think of disillusion or humiliation or failure. And yet – Promise me you'll never tell him. Well, it came into my head just as he was holding me in his arms and looking into my eyes, that perhaps we only had our heroic ideas because we're so fond of reading Byron and Pushkin, and because we were so delighted with the opera that season at Bucharest. Real life is so seldom like that, indeed never, as far as I knew it then. Only think, mother, I doubted him: I wondered whether all his heroic qualities and his soldiership might not prove mere imagination when he went into a real battle. I had an uneasy fear that he might cut a poor figure there beside all those clever officers from the Tsar's court.

I was only a prosaic little coward. Oh, to think that it was all true, that Sergius is just as splendid and noble as he looks! That the world is really a glorious world for women who can see its glory and men who can act its romance! What happiness! What unspeakable fulfilment!

FANNY'S FIRST PLAY by GEORGE BERNARD SHAW (1916)

(The prologue of the play is performed by the actress who plays the character, Margaret Knox. Margaret has written a play and addresses the audience).

Fanny:

We're going to act a play. I shall be in it.
Thank you for that applause. But – just a minute –
Would you mind very much if I explained to you
What wouldn't otherwise be very plain to you:
That is, why – though the play's won worldwide fame –
The author's given it such a funny name!
Fanny's First Play! It's catching. Lots of pence in it.
But at first sight there doesn't seem much sense in it.
But don't make up your minds there isn't any:
It's really Fanny's play; and I am Fanny.
I wrote the play. It was very first.
(I had to write it or I should have burst:
I couldn't help it). Now, from what you've read of it,
You know, perhaps, that all the critics said of it
That, though my first might fairly good be reckoned,
Heaven forbid that I should write a second!
That was a nasty one; they thought it witty;
But I felt nothing for the fools but pity;
For stalls and pit to praise my play united;
And now, I'll tell you how I came to write it.

In childhood's sunny days, I, by an Aunt of mine,
Was taken – prematurely – to the pantomime.
From that time forth, each evening I would be at her:
"Take me again, dear Auntie, to the theatre".
'Twas thus I first on Shakespeare's golden page struck.
The natural result was, I got stage struck.
I loved the playhouse; after my first bout of it,
I dared my family to keep me out of it.
I went and went and went, until, alas!
Something most unexpected came to pass.

I loved the actors; copied all their ways;
But oh! I got so tired of the plays.
At first, I liked them. All my soul was stored with them;
But, in a year or so, I got quite bored with them.
Just think! In real life what is it touches us?
Stories about ourselves, not about Duchesses.
Why are stage lovers' speeches drowned by coughs?
Because we're all tired of their being toffs.
As to the titled heroine, I'd banish her,
But when I hinted at it to the manager,
He said," To put the Duchess on the shelf,
Just write a play and act in it yourself".

Ladies and Gentlemen: I all but kissed him:
In fact, I threw a kiss – like that – but missed him.
I wrote the play: Fanny's First, at your service.
You'll see me act in it. Oh, I'm so nervous.
You won't expect me in the First Act, will you?
But in the second, I shall simply thrrrill you.
The Third, you must especially attend to.
If you don't like my part, oh, please pretend to.
You see, unless you think it rather funny,
You won't feel you've had value for your money.
I really must break off: it's downright wrong
Making all this up as I go along;
Besides, I've got to change. I look too rowdy.
Business folk like their daughter to be dowdy.
I'll make myself so plain, you'll all despise me,
I'm sure not one of you will recognize me.
But beauty's nothing: common people love it:
But you're not common people: you're above it.
I knew you were. You all look quite resigned.
Well, since you've been so very, very kind,
My poor looks shall not be much diminished.
Thank you for hearing me. (*to the prompter*).
Ring up. I've finished.

FANNY'S FIRST PLAY by GEORGE BERNARD SHAW (1916)

(In Act 1, Dora Delaney comes to visit Mr & Mrs Gilbey to inform them about their son, Bobby, who has been detained at the police station. Dora is a lively, local London girl and is of a different class to the Gilbeys).

Dora:

Oh, ain't we impatient! Well, it does you credit, old dear. And you needn't fuss: there's no disgrace. Bobby behaved like a perfect gentleman. Besides, it was all my fault. I'll own it: I took too much champagne. I was not what you might call drunk; but I was bright, and a little beyond myself; and—I'll confess it—I wanted to show off before Bobby, because he was a bit taken by a woman on the stage; and she was pretending to be game for anything. You see you've brought Bobby up too strict; and when he gets loose there's no holding him. He does enjoy life more than any lad I ever met.

Well, it was a beautiful moonlight night; and we couldn't get a cab on the nod; so, we started to walk, very jolly, you know: arm in arm, and dancing along, singing and all that. When we came into Jamaica Square, there was a young copper on point duty at the corner. I says to Bob: "Dearie boy: is it a bargain about the squiffer if I make Joe sprint for you?" "Anything you like, darling," says he: "I love you." I put on my best company manners and stepped up to the copper. "If you please, sir," says I, "can you direct me to Carrickmines Square?" I was so genteel, and talked so sweet, that he fell to it like a bird. "I never heard of any such Square in these parts," he says. "Then," says I, "what a very silly little officer you must be!"; and I gave his helmet a chuck behind that knocked it over his eyes, and did a bunk.

Holy Joe did one too all right: he sprinted faster than he ever did in college, I bet, the old dear. He got clean off, too. Just as he was overtaking me half-way down the square, we heard the whistle; and at the sound of it he drew away like a streak of lightning; and that was the last I saw of him. I was copped in the Dock Road myself: rotten luck, wasn't it? I tried the innocent and genteel and all the rest; but Bobby's hat done me in.

Only fancy! He stopped to laugh at the copper! He thought the copper would see the joke, poor lamb. He was arguing about it when the two that took me came along to find out what the whistle was for, and brought me with them. Of course, I swore I'd never seen him before in my life; but there he was in my hat and I in his. The cops were very spiteful and laid it on for all they were worth: drunk and disorderly and assaulting the police and all that. I got fourteen days without the option, because you see—well, the fact is, I'd done it before, and been warned. Bobby was a first offender and had the option; but the dear boy had no money left and wouldn't give you away by telling his name; and anyhow he couldn't have brought himself to buy himself off and leave me there; so, he's doing his time. Well, it was two forty shillingses; and I've only twenty-eight shillings in the world, if I pawn my clothes. I shan't be able to earn any more. So, I can't pay the fine and get him out; but if you'll stand three pounds, I'll stand one; and that'll do it. If you'd like to be very kind and nice you could pay the lot; but I can't deny that it was my fault; so, I won't press you.

FANNY'S FIRST PLAY by GEORGE BERNARD SHAW (1916)

(In Act 2, Margaret Knox is trying to explain to her mother why she has been locked up in prison).

Margaret:

You see, it's all real to me. I've suffered it. I've been shoved and bullied. I've had my arms twisted. I've been made scream with pain in other ways. I've been flung into a filthy cell with a lot of other poor wretches as if I were a sack of coals being emptied into a cellar. And the only difference between me and the others was that I hit back. Yes, I did. And I did worse. I wasn't ladylike. I cursed. I called names. I heard words that I didn't even know that I knew, coming out of my mouth just as if somebody else had spoken them. The policeman repeated them in court. The magistrate said he could hardly believe it. The policeman held out his hand with his two teeth in it that I knocked out. I said it was all right; that I had heard myself using those words quite distinctly; and that I had taken the good conduct prize for three years running at school. The poor old gentleman put me back for the missionary to find out who I was, and to ascertain the state of my mind. I wouldn't tell, of course, for your sakes at home here; and I wouldn't say I was sorry, or apologize to the policeman, or compensate him or anything of that sort. I wasn't sorry. The one thing that gave me any satisfaction was getting in that smack on his mouth; and I said so. So, the missionary reported that I seemed hardened and that no doubt I would tell who I was after a day in prison. Then I was sentenced. So now you see I'm not a bit the sort of girl you thought me. I'm not a bit the sort of girl I thought myself. And I don't know what sort of person you really are, or what sort of person father really is. I wonder what he would say or do if he had an angry brute of a policeman twisting his arm with one hand and rushing him along by the nape of his neck with the other. He couldn't whirl his leg like a windmill and knock a policeman down by a glorious kick on the helmet. Oh, if they'd all fought as we two fought, we'd have beaten them.

FANNY'S FIRST PLAY by GEORGE BERNARD SHAW (1916)

(In Act 2, Margaret Knox is trying to explain to her mother why she has been locked up in prison).

Margaret:

It began on the boat-race night.

The meeting at the great Salvation Festival at the Albert Hall got on my nerves, somehow. It was the singing, I suppose: you know I love singing a good swinging hymn; and I felt it was ridiculous to go home in the bus after we had been singing so wonderfully about climbing up the golden stairs to heaven. I wanted more music—more happiness—more life. I wanted some comrade who felt as I did. I felt exalted: it seemed mean to be afraid of anything: after all, what could anyone do to me against my will? I suppose I was a little mad: at all events, I got out of the bus at Piccadilly Circus, because there was a lot of light and excitement there. I walked to Leicester Square; and went into a great theatre. It was very stuffy; and I didn't like the people much, because they didn't seem to be enjoying themselves; but the stage was splendid and the music lovely. I saw that Frenchman, Monsieur Duvallet, standing against a barrier, smoking a cigarette. He seemed quite happy; and he was nice and sailor-like. I went and stood beside him, hoping he would speak to me. He did, just as if he had known me for years. We got on together like old friends. He asked me would I have some champagne; and I said it would cost too much, but that I would give anything for a dance. I longed to join the people on the stage and dance with them: one of them was the most beautiful dancer I ever saw. He told me he had come there to see her, and that when it was over, we could go somewhere where there was dancing. So, we went to a place where there was a band in a gallery and the floor cleared for dancing. Very few people danced: the women only wanted to show off their dresses; but we danced and danced until a lot of them joined in. We got quite reckless; and we had had champagne after all. I never enjoyed anything so much. But at last, it got spoilt by the Oxford and Cambridge students up for the boat race. They got drunk; and they began to smash things; and the police came in. Then it was quite horrible. The students fought with the police; and the police suddenly got quite brutal, and began to throw everybody downstairs.They attacked the women, who were not doing anything, and treated them just as roughly as they had treated the students. Duvallet got indignant and remonstrated with a policeman, who was shoving a woman though she was going quietly as fast as she could. The policeman flung the woman through the door and then turned on Duvallet. It was then that Duvallet swung his leg like a windmill and knocked the policeman down. And then three policemen rushed at him and carried him out by the arms and legs face downwards. Two more attacked me and gave me a shove to the door. That quite maddened me. I just got in one good bang on the mouth of one of them. All the rest was dreadful. I was rushed through the streets to the police station. They kicked me with their knees; they twisted my arms; they taunted and insulted me; they called me vile names; and I told them what I thought of them, and provoked them to do their worst. There's one good thing about being hard hurt: it makes you sleep. I slept in that filthy cell with all the other drunks sounder than I should have slept at home. I can't describe how I felt next morning: it was hideous; but the police were quite jolly; and everybody said it was a bit of English fun, and talked about last year's boat-race night when it had been a great deal worse. I was black and blue and sick and wretched. But the strange thing was that I wasn't sorry; and I'm not sorry. And I don't feel that I did anything wrong, really. [*She rises and stretches her arms with a large liberating breath*] Now that it's all over I'm rather proud of it; though I know now that I'm not a lady; but whether that's because we're only shopkeepers, or because nobody's really a lady except when they're treated like ladies, I don't know. [*She throws herself into a corner of the sofa*].

I don't understand it myself. The prayer meeting set me free, somehow. I should never have done it if it were not for the prayer meeting.

SAINT JOAN by GEORGE BERNARD SHAW (1923)

(*Scene 111, the time is 1429 on the banks of the river Loire. Joan has found Dunois. She is wearing armor and rushes in, in a blazing rage*).

Joan:

Be you the bastard of Orleans?

My troops are miles behind. They have cheated me. They have brought me to the wrong side of the river. Why? The English are on the other side. But Orleans is on the other side. We must fight the English there. How can we cross the river? In God's name, then, let us cross the bridge, and fall on them. Your older and wiser heads are fatheads: they have made a fool of you; and now they want to make a fool of me too, bringing me to the wrong side of the river. Do you not know that I bring you better help than ever came to any general or any town? Which is the way to the bridge? Is this a time for patience? Our enemy is at our gates; and here we stand doing nothing. Oh, why are you not fighting? Listen to me: I will deliver you from fear.

God did not give them the land under those forts: they stole it from Him. He gave it to us. I will take those forts. Our men will take them. I will lead them. I will not look back to see whether anyone is following me.

I will never take a husband. A man in Toul took an action against me for breach of promise; but I never promised him. I am a soldier: I do not want to be thought of as a woman. I will not dress as a woman. I do not care for the things women care for. They dream of lovers, and of money. I dream of leading a charge, and of placing the big guns. You soldiers do not know how to use the big guns: you think you can win battles with a great noise and smoke. But you cannot fight stone walls with horses: you must have guns, and much bigger guns too. I will be first up the ladder when we reach the fort, Bastard. I dare you to follow me.

I am not a daredevil: I am a servant of God. My sword is sacred: I found it behind the altar in the church of St Catherine, where God hid it for me; and I may not strike a blow with it. My heart is full of courage, not of anger. I will lead; and your men will follow: that is all I can do. But I must do it: you shall not stop me.

Make rafts and put big guns on them; and let your men cross to us. The English will not yield to prayers: they understand nothing but hard knocks and slashes. I will not go to church until we have beaten them. I will tell St Catherine: she will make God give me a west wind. Quick: show me the way to the church.

SAINT JOAN by GEORGE BERNARD SHAW (1923)

(Scene 6, Rouen, 30th May 1431. A great hall in the castle is arranged for a trial. The Bishop and the Inquisitor are judges. There are also canons, doctors of law and theology and Dominican monks. The prisoner's stool is on the left).

<u>Joan:</u>

Sign? That means to write my name. I cannot write. Do not trouble. I will sign it. It is plain enough, sir.

Perpetual imprisonment! Am I not then to be set free?

Give me that writing. (*She rushes to the paper; and tears it into fragments).* Light your fire: do you think I dread it as much as the life of a rat in a hole? My voices were right.

They told me you were fools, and that I was not to listen to your fine words nor trust to your charity. You promised me my life; but you lied. You think that life is nothing but not being stone dead. It is not the bread and water I fear: I can live on bread: when have I asked for more? It is no hardship to drink water if the water be clean. But to shut me from the light of the sky and the sight of the fields and flowers; to chain my feet so that I can never again ride with the soldiers nor climb the hills; to make me breathe foul damp darkness, and keep from me everything that brings me back to the love of God when your wickedness and foolishness tempt me to hate Him: I could do without my warhorse; I could drag about in a skirt; I could let the banners and the trumpets and the knights and soldiers pass me and leave me behind as they leave the other women, if only I could still hear the wind in the trees, the larks in the sunshine, the young lambs crying though the healthy frost, and the blessed, blessed church bells that send my angel voices floating to me on the wind. But without these things I cannot live; and by your wanting to take them away from me, or from any human creature, I know that your counsel is of the devil, and that mine is of God. Gods ways are not your ways. I am His child, and you are not fit that I should live among you.

THE DARK LADY OF THE SONNETS by GEORGE BERNARD SHAW (1910)

(This is a short comic play. William Shakespeare meets Queen Elizabeth 1, purely by accident, and tries to persuade her to form a National theatre for the nation. Queen Elizabeth berates Shakespeare).

Elizabeth I:

You have an overweening conceit of yourself, sir, that displeases your Queen. I bid you remember that I do not suffer persons of your degree to presume too far.

Are there not theatres enough on the Bankside and in Blackfriars?

Master Shakespeare: I will speak of this matter to the Lord Treasurer.

Master Shakespeare: you speak sooth; yet cannot I in any wise mend it. I dare not offend my unruly Puritans by making so lewd a place as the playhouse a public charge; and there be a thousand things to be done in this London of mine before your poetry can have its penny from the general purse. I tell thee, Master Will, it will be three hundred years and more before my subjects learn that man cannot live by bread alone, but by every word that cometh from the mouth of those whom God inspires. By that time, you and I will be dust beneath the feet of the horses, if indeed there be any horses then, and men be still riding instead of flying. Now it may be that by then your works will be dust also.

But of this I am certain (for I know my countrymen) that until every other country in the Christian world, even to barbarian Muscovy and the hamlets of the boorish Germans, have its playhouse at the public charge, England will never adventure. And she will adventure then only because it is her desire to be ever in the fashion, and do humbly and dutifully whatsoever she seeth everybody else doing. In the mean time you must content yourself as best you can by the playing of those two pieces which you give out as the most damnable ever writ, but which your countrymen, I warn you, will swear are the best you have ever done. But this, I will say, that if I could speak across the ages to our descendants, I should heartily recommend them to fulfil your wish; for the Scottish minstrel hath well said that he that maketh the songs of a nation is mightier than he that maketh its laws; and the same may well be true of plays and interludes. And now sir, we are upon the hour when it better beseems a virgin queen to be abed than to converse alone with the naughtiest of her subjects. Ho there! Who keeps ward on the queen's lodgings tonight?

(The warder announces that it is him).

See that you keep it better in future. You have let pass a most dangerous gallant even to the very door of our royal chamber. Lead him forth; and bring me word when he is safely locked out; for I shall scarce dare disrobe until the palace gates are between us.

PYGMALION by GEORGE BERNARD SHAW (1912)

(This scene takes place towards the end of the play, Eliza takes her revenge on Professor Higgins).

Eliza Doolittle.

Oh, I'm only a squashed cabbage leaf –

But I owe so much to you that I should be very unhappy if you forgot me. It's not because you paid for my dresses. I know you are generous to everybody with money. But it was from you that I learnt really nice manners; and that is what makes one a lady, isn't it? You see it was so very difficult for me with the example of Professor Higgins always before me. I was brought up to be just like him, unable to control myself, and using bad language on the slightest provocation. And I should never have known that ladies and gentlemen didn't behave like that if you hadn't been there. I didn't mean it, when I was a flower girl. It was only my way. But you see I did it; and that's what makes the difference after all. But do you know what began my real education? Your calling me Miss Doolittle that day when I first came to Wimpole Street. That was the beginning of self-respect for me. And there were a hundred little things you never noticed, because they came naturally to you. Things about standing up and taking off your hat and opening doors

Yes: things that showed you thought and felt about me as if I were something better than a scullery-maid; though of course I know you would have been just the same to a scullery-maid if she had been let into the drawing-room. You never took off your boots in the dining-room when I was there. It made such a difference to me that you didn't do it. You see, really and truly, apart from the things anyone can pick up (the dressing and the proper way of speaking, and so on) the difference between a lady and a flower girl is not how she behaves, but how she's treated. I shall always be a flower girl to Professor Higgins, because he always treats me as a flower girl, and always will; but I know I can be a lady to you, because you always treat me as a lady and always will.

(*To Mr Pickering*) I should like you to call me Eliza, now, if you would. (*To Professor Higgins*). And I should like Professor Higgins to call me Miss Doolittle.

PYGMALION by GEORGE BERNARD SHAW
(1912)

(Eliza *snatches up the slippers, and hurling them at Professor Higgins, one after the other. Her training is now over or as she calls it, 'their little experiment' and she feels that they are discarding her like an old shoe).*

Eliza:

There are your slippers. And there. Take your slippers; and may you never have a day's luck with them!

I've won your bet for you, haven't I? That's enough for you.

Why did I throw those slippers? Because I wanted to smash your face. I'd like to kill you, you selfish brute. Why didn't you leave me where you picked me out of – in the gutter? You thank God it's all over, and that now you can throw me back again there, do you?

(Eliza gives a suffocated scream of fury, and instinctively darts her nails at his face. Prof. Higgins throws her roughly into the easy-chair. She is crushed by his superior strength and weight).

What's to become of me? What's to become of me?
You don't care. I know you don't care. You wouldn't care if I was dead. I'm nothing to you – not so much as them slippers.
Those slippers. I didn't think it made any difference now.
Nothing more for you to worry about. Oh God! I wish I was dead.
I don't understand. I'm too ignorant.

I heard your prayers. 'Thank God it's all over'!

What am I fit for? What have you left me fit for? Where am I to go? What am I to do? What's to become of me? We were above that at the corner of Tottenham Court Road. I sold flowers. I didn't sell myself. Now you've made a lady of me I'm not fit to sell anything else. I wish you'd left me where you found me. What else am I to do?

Before you go, sir – Do my clothes belong to me or to Colonel Pickering? He might want them for the next girl you pick up to experiment on. All I want to know is whether anything belongs to me. My own clothes were burnt. I want to know what I may take away with me. I don't want to be accused of stealing. I'm only a common ignorant girl; and in my station I have to be careful. There can't be any feelings between the like of you and the like of me. Please will you tell me what belongs to me and what doesn't? (*She takes off the jewels she is wearing*). Will you take these to your room and keep them safe? I don't want to run the risk of their being missing. This ring isn't yours. It's the jeweller's: it's the one you bought me in Brighton. I don't want it now.

MRS WARREN'S PROFESSION by GEORGE BERNARD SHAW (1902)

(In Act 2, Vivie confronts her mother about her past. Vivie adopts a very moralistic approach to her mother's past behaviour. She demands to know who her father is).

Vivie:

Do you expect that we shall be much together? You and I, I mean? Do you think my way of life would suit you? I doubt it. Has it really never occurred to you, mother, that I have a way of life like other people?

Who are you? What are you? Everybody knows my reputation, my social standing, and the profession I intend to pursue. I know nothing about you. What is that way of life which you invite me to share with you and Sir George Crofts, pray?

Well, let us drop the subject until you are better able to face it. You want some good walks and a little lawn tennis to set you up. You are shockingly out of condition: you were not able to manage twenty yards uphill today without stopping to pant; and your wrists are mere rolls of fat. Look at mine. Now pray don't begin to cry. Anything but that. I really cannot stand whimpering. I will go out of the room if you do.

Are you my mother? Then where are our relatives? My father? Our family friends? You claim the rights of a mother: the right to call me fool and child; to speak to me as no woman in authority over me at college dare speak to me; to dictate my way of life; and to force on me the acquaintance of a brute whom anyone can see to be the most vicious sort of London man about town. Before I give myself the trouble to resist such claims, I may as well find out whether they have any real existence. Who was my father? I have a right to know; and you know very well that I have that right. You can refuse to tell me, if you please; but if you do, you will see the last of me tomorrow morning. How can I feel sure that I may not have the contaminated blood of that brutal water in my veins?

MRS WARREN'S PROFESSION by GEORGE BERNARD SHAW (1902)

(Mrs Warren is talking to her daughter, Vivie. She tries to explain the difficulties of her past. Mrs Warren has made her wealth as a former prostitute and brothel owner).

Mrs Warren:

What is any respectable girl brought up to do but to catch some rich man's fancy and get the benefit of his money by marrying him? - as if a marriage ceremony could make any difference in the right or wrong of the thing! Oh, the hypocrisy of the world makes me sick! Liz and I had to work and save and calculate just like other people; elseways, we should be as poor as any good-for-nothing drunken waster of a woman that thinks her luck will last forever. I despise such people: they've no character; and if there's a thing I hate in a woman, it's want of character.

Everybody dislikes having to work and make money, but they have to do it all the same. I'm sure I've often pitied a poor girl, tired out and in low spirits, having to try to please some man that she doesn't care two straws for – some half-drunken fool that thinks he's making himself agreeable when he's teasing and worrying and disgusting a woman so that hardly any money could pay her for putting up with it. But she has to bear with the disagreeable and take the rough with the smooth, just like a nurse in a hospital or anyone else. It's not work that any woman would do for pleasure, goodness knows; though to hear the pious people talk you would suppose it was a bed of roses.

Of course, it's worthwhile to a poor girl, if she can resist temptation and is good-looking and well conducted and sensible. It's far better than any other employment open to her. I always thought that it oughtn't to be. It can't be right, Vivie, that there shouldn't be better opportunities for women. I stick to that: it's wrong. But it is so, right or wrong; and a girl must make the best of it. But of course, it's not worthwhile for a lady. If you took to it, you'd be a fool; but I should have been a fool if I'd taken to anything else.

THE FOREIGN DRAMATISTS

CARLO GOLDONI

GEORGES FEYDEAU

FEDERICO GARCIA LORCA

JEAN ANOUILH

CARLO GOLDONI
ITALIAN DRAMATIST
1707-1793

A Venetian dramatist who wrote some of Italy's best-known plays. He writes in the style of commedia dell'arte and his writing his full of satire, wit and humour. He wrote mostly comedies but there were a few tragicomedies, opera libretti and some poetry. His most successful plays are: The Servant of Two Masters, The Two Venetian Twins, The Liar, The Boors, The True Friend, The Lovers and The Mistress of the Inn.

MIRANDOLINA BY CARLO GOLDONI (1751)

(Mirandolina is a comic opera, otherwise known as 'The Mistress of the Inn. Mirandolina is an attractive inn-keeper who is courted by various well-heeled suitors at her home in Florence. The two suitors battle with each other for her affections but Mirandolina is fickle and dismisses them. She has another admirer, the womanising, Knight of Ripafratta whom she sees as a bit of a challenge. However, Mirandolina ultimately ends up marrying her servant Fabrizius, as he is far more loyal than her other suitors. Ripafratta is not amused).

Mirandolina:

Marquis Empty Pockets, that fine fellow, wants to marry me? Yes, if you wanted to, you'd find a little difficulty. I like the good things of life, but have no use for the disagreeable. If all who said they wanted me, had married me, oh how many husbands I'd have had. Everyone who has come to this inn has fallen in love with me, everyone has made desperate love to me, and many a one has offered to marry me on the spot. And as to that Cavalier, who is as rough as a bear, why does he treat me so brusquely? He's the first guest who's come to my inn who hasn't been delighted to be in my society. I don't say that everyone has fallen in love at first sight, but to despise me so, is something that makes me angry. He a woman hater? He can't bear the sight of them? Poor fool! Probably he hasn't found the one who knows how to handle him. But he shall find her. He shall. And who knows that he hasn't found her. I'm going to enter the lists with him. Those who run after me, soon bore me. Nobility has no weight with me. I value riches, but not nobility. My whole delight is in seeing myself served, desired, and adored. That is my weakness, as it is the weakness of almost all women. I'm not thinking of marrying any one; I don't need anyone; I live honestly and I enjoy my freedom. I treat everyone well, but I'll never fall in love with anyone. I like to make fun of those exaggerated ardent lovers, and I want to use all my skill to conquer, strike down and shake to their depths these cruel and hard hearts which are the enemies of us who are the best thing that beautiful mother nature has produced in this world.

MIRANDOLINA BY CARLO GOLDONI (1751)

(Mirandolina is a comic opera, otherwise known as 'The Mistress of the Inn. Mirandolina is an attractive inn-keeper who is courted by various well-heeled suitors at her home in Florence. The two suitors battle with each other for her affections but Mirandolina is fickle and dismisses them. She has another admirer, the womanising, Knight of Ripafratta whom she sees as a bit of a challenge. However, Mirandolina ultimately ends up marrying her servant Fabrizius, as he is far more loyal than her other suitors. In this scene, the Marquis of Foliporli wants to marry Mirandolina.).

Mirandolina:

What a cheek! The high and mighty Marquis of Foliporli wants to marry me., does he? Well, there is one insuperable obstacle – I won't have him! If I married everyone who asked me I'd have been married many times. Almost every man who comes to this inn seems to fall in love with me. And quite a number of them propose to me too and want to marry me immediately.

These Men really get on my nerves. I have no interest in high status. As for wealth – well, it's nice as far as it goes. I like being served, worshipped and adored. It's my little weakness. Come to think of it, it's probably most women's little weakness. But I don't want to get married, I don't need anyone. I am free and like to enjoy myself. I have fun when I want and I have no intention of falling in love. And as for the Knight of Ripafratta, he's as cultured and rude as a hippopotamus. What's his problem? Does he hate women? Can he not bear to look at them? He hasn't yet met the woman who knows how to make him look at her. But he will! I could twist him round my little finger!

GEORGES FEYDEAU
FRENCH PLAYWRIGHT
1862-1921

The Parisien, Georges Feydeau is best known for his farces, covering themes of mistaken identity and infidelity. His titles include: A Pig in a Poke, The Edward Affair, The Ribbon, The Lady from Maxim's, Josephine's Letter, The Duchess of the Folies-Bergeres, A Flea in her Ear, I Don't Cheat on my Husband and Who's My Wife?

HOTEL PARADISO by GEORGES FEYDEAU (1894)

(This scene is from Act 3 of one of Georges Feydeau's hilarious farces. Hotel Paradiso is a disreputable hotel in Paris. Angelique is the overbearing wife of Benedict Boniface).

Angelique:

Boniface! ... Boniface! Boniface!
Oh, Boniface! ... Benedict! My dear! (*She has an enormous black eye*). Oh, what a night! *What* a night! (*taking off her coat*).
Benedict! Benedict! Where *are* you?

It's me, my love! Come here, quickly! I am only just alive!

(*To herself*) Wait until he hears what happened to me! Wait till he hears how near to disaster I've been while he was sleeping peacefully in his bed! Benedict! Come quickly!

(*Benedict appears*).

Ah! Benedict! I'm so happy to see you! Oh, what a night! What a night! Oh, Boniface, do you realise, you very nearly lost me! Word of honour! Oh, my dear! I had an accident ... a ghastly accident, which nearly deprived you of my person forever! Oh! my own dear one! Well, as you know, I hired a carriage to take me to my sister's in Versailles. At first everything went well, and there we were, trotting along all three of us – Yes, the driver, the horse and me! Suddenly, as we were going through the gates of Paris, the horse was frightened by a train whistle ... and it bolted!

Oh, my love! ... You've come in just at the right moment! I think I must be going mad! ... I must have forgotten how to read ... Look at this! Oh no! It says ... it says ... No, it's too frightful! Read it! (*She gives him the letter*). Read it! Read it!

Yes! ... Me! ... Me! ... It says I was caught last night with Monsieur Cot! I was doing nothing with Monsieur Cot ... nothing, I promise you .. This is madness!

Benedict! You're hurting me … you're hurting me terribly! You can't want me to confess to something that isn't true! But it's a lie, I tell you, a foul lie! I didn't go to the Paradiso. Never! … Never, never I tell you! … I didn't even know it *was* in the rue de Provence … Who told *you* it was in the Rue de Provence? I swear I'm telling you the truth … everything that happened … the runaway horse … the vegetable marrows … the peasants who rescued me! I was whirled away to … I don't know where … miles away! … I should have asked, I know, but with the shock of it all … I never thought … But wait! Cot! … What about Cot? Since he is named too, perhaps he will be able to tell you … to explain. Oh, you Spirits Above … who know the Unsullied Truth, look down and justify me before this Man!

FEDERICO GARCIA LORCA
SPANISH DRAMATIST
1898-1936

Lorca was a poet and playwright. His writing is often symbolic and full of poetry and song. His work explores themes of love and loss. The countryside and Spanish life features in his work. His best known plays are: Yerma, Blood Wedding, The House of Bernarda Alba, Dona Rosita & Mariana Pineda.

YERMA BY FEDERICO GARCIA LORCA (1934)

(*Yerma goes out in to the countryside to meet an old pagan woman. She has been unable to become pregnant by her husband. She is desperate for advice on how she might conceive a child*).

Yerma:

Good day. I'm Enrique the shepherd's daughter. I'd like to ask you something. I've been wanting to talk about things with an older woman for a long time. Because I have to know. I have to. And you can tell me …

You know what it is. Why am I barren? Am I to spend the best years of my life looking after the fowls or ironing dainty curtains to put up at my little window? No. You just tell me what I have to do and I'll do it, whatever it is, even if you tell me to stick needles into the tenderest part of my eyes.

Do I love my husband? I don't know. Once – when Victor …. He put his arm round my waist, and I couldn't say a word to him because I couldn't speak. Another time – it was Victor again; when I was fourteen – he was a big, strong boy; he picked me up in his arms to get across a ditch, and I started trembling so much my teeth chattered. But then I've always been very modest. With my husband, it's not the same. My father gave him to me and I took him. Gladly. That's the absolute truth. Then the moment I got engaged to him I began to think … about having children. And I could see myself in his eyes. Yes, but what I saw was myself very tiny and easy to handle, just as if I myself were my own little girl.

I think about many things, all sorts of things, and I'm quite sure that my child is meant to make those things come true. It was for his sake that I first gave myself to my husband, and it's so that he can be born that I go on giving myself, but I never do it for pleasure. I'm filling up with hatred. You tell me, am I the one who's to blame? Are you supposed to want a man just for being a man and for nothing else? If that's all, what are you going to think in bed when he leaves you staring miserably up at the ceiling while he turns his back on you and goes to sleep? Am I supposed to go on thinking about him or about the glorious new life that might come out of my body? I don't know, but you tell me; for pity's sake, tell me!

Country girls like me find every door closed against them. All we get are hints and gestures because they say that all these things are not for us to know. And you're the same, you won't speak either; you put on the airs of a doctor who knows it all, and then you won't give water to a woman who's dying of thirst.

DONA ROSITA by FEDERICO GARCIA LORCA (1935)

(Rosita is talking to the Nephew. The two cousins have fallen in love and have promised to marry. However, in this scene, he comes to Rosita's garden to break the news that he has to go away. She is heart-broken. He promises to return, which he never does, and unfortunately, poor Rosita is unable to marry anyone else due to her commitment to be only his).

Rosita:

When your eyes met mine, cousin,
They did so treacherously.
When your hands gave me flowers, cousin,
They did so deceitfully.
And now, still young, you are leaving me
To the nightingale's sad song.
You, whom I loved so truly.
Can only do me this wrong.
How can you leave me so cruelly,
Like the strings of a lute struck dumb?

One night on my jasmine balcony
I lay asleep and dreaming,
And dreamt I saw two cherubs attend
A rose sick with yearning.

Her colour was the palest white,
But she turned the deepest red.

By nature fragile and tender,
Her burning petals bled,
Till, wounded by love's assault,
The rose lay cold and dead.
So I, innocent cousin,
In the garden of myrtle walking,
To the fountain offered my paleness,
To the soft wind my longing.

Like a tender, foolish gazelle,
I dared to look on you lovingly,
At once my heart was pierced
By needles of quivering agony.
Its wounds as red as wallflower
Began to bleed fatally.

When the spirit's left alone,
Love drips its poison slowly.
With earth and salt it shall weave
The shroud that will soon clothe me.

My dream is to see you come, cousin,
At night through Granada to me,
When the light's full of salt, cousin,
From longing for the sea.
A lemon grove of yellow,
Jasmine that's white and bloodless,
Stones that kill with their hardness,
All will stop your progress,
And nards spinning like whirlpools
Will fill my house with madness.
Will you ever come back?

DONA ROSITA by FEDERICO GARCIA LORCA (1935)

(The mother of the three spinster girls, acquaintances of Rosita's aunt and uncle are at the family home to celebrate Rosita's birthday).

Mother:

Happy Birthday! (*She kisses Rosita*).

Well, girls. Have you brought the card? I've never lacked taste! Only money!

Now, girls, I'm among friends here. There's no one can hear us. You know perfectly well that since my poor husband was taken from me, I've performed real miracles in order to manage on a pension. I fancy I can still hear the father of these girls when, generous gentleman that he was, he used to tell me; 'Henrietta, spend, spend, spend! I'm earning decent money now'. Ah well, those days are gone! But even so, we've managed to keep our position in society. What agony I've gone through, madam, so that my girls shouldn't be deprived of hats! I've shed many a tear, sighed many a sigh on account of a ribbon or an arrangement of curls! Those feathers and wires have cost me many a sleepless night!

But, it's the truth, my child. We can't spend at all beyond our means. Many's the time I say to them: 'Now, what do you really want, dear girls? An egg for breakfast or a chair when you promenade? They all reply together: 'A chair'.

But then, what else could they say? We may have to eat potatoes or a bunch of grapes, but we've still got our Mongolian cape, or a painted parasol, or a poplinette blouse with all the trimmings. There's just no alternative. Even so, it's such an ordeal! My eyes fill with tears when I see them competing with girls who have money.

THE HOUSE OF BERNARD ALBA by FEDERICO GARCIA LORCA (1945)

(*Adela has just entered. Martirio, Adela's sister, has been calling for her. Adela appears. Her hair is somewhat dishevelled. She has been with Pepe El Romano*).

Adela:

Why are you looking for me? Who are you to tell me what to do?

This is only the beginning. I had the strength to take action. The spirit and the courage that you haven't got. Under this roof I saw death, and I went to get what was mine, what belonged to me.

He wanted her money, but his eyes were always on me. You know even better than I do that he doesn't love her. You know it's me he loves because you've seen him with me. He loves *me*, he loves *me*. That's why you want to stop me going with him. You don't care if he puts his arms around a woman he doesn't love. Neither do I. It's all right for him to spend a hundred years with Angustias. But, if he puts his arms around me, you can't bear it, because you love him too, you love him!

Martirio, oh Martirio, it's not my fault. There's no way out of this. One of us must sink, the other swim. Pepe El Romano is mine. He takes me into the reed-beds by the river. I can't stand the horrors of this house anymore, not after feeling the taste of his mouth. I'll be whatever he wants me to be. The whole village will be against me, pointing their fiery fingers and burning me up, I'll be hounded by those that call themselves respectable, and in front of them all I'll put on the crown of thorns worn by every woman who's loved by a married man.

Yes, Let's go to bed, let's leave him to marry Angustias. I don't care anymore. But I'll go and live in a little house by myself where he can come and see me when he wants to, whenever he feels like it. Oh, you won't stop me, you're feeble; I could bring a bucking stallion to his knees just with the strength in my little finger.

They tell us we should love our sisters. God must have abandoned me to dwell in darkness, because I look at you as if I'd never seen you before.

(*A whistle is heard, and Adela runs towards the door to the yard, but Martirio bars her way*).

Get away from the door. Get away! Let me go! Nobody but Pepe tells me what to do.

JEAN ANOUILH
FRENCH DRAMATIST
1910-1987

Anouilh wrote a wide range of plays and was versatile in his style of writing. His most famous play being 'Antigone'. His later work became much darker where he explored the differences between good and evil. His plays include: Antigone, Leocadia, Ring Round the Moon, The Lark, The Waltz of the Toreadors, Becket & The Fighting Cock. All of his work is theatrical in nature and rejects both Naturalism and Realism.

ANTIGONE by JEAN ANOUILH (1942)

(Antigone is talking to her uncle, King Creon. She is determined to bury her brother at any cost).

Antigone:

And what will my happiness be like? What kind of a happy woman will Antigone grow into? What base things will she have to do, day after day, in order to snatch her own little scrap of happiness? Tell me – who will she have to lie to? Smile at? Sell herself to? Who will she have to avert her eyes from, and leave to die?
I won't be quiet! I want to know what I have to do to be happy! Now, right away, because now is when I have to choose. You say life's so wonderful. I want to know what I have to do to live.
I love a Haemon who's tough and young … A Haemon who's demanding and loyal, like me. But if that life of yours, that happiness of yours, are going to pass over him and erode him – if he's going to become just a conventional spouse and learn to say yes like the rest – then, no, I don't love Haemon anymore!
I know what I'm saying, all right! It's just that you don't understand. I suddenly see you as you were when you were fifteen! Helpless, but thinking you're important. All life has added are those furrows in your face, that fat around your waist!

You know I'm right? Don't you think I can see it in your eyes? You know I'm right, but you'll never admit it because you're trying to defend that happiness of yours – like a dog crouching over a bone.

You disgust me, all of you, you and your happiness! And your life, that has to be loved at any price. But I want everything, now! And to the full! Or else I decline the offer, lock, stock and barrel! I want to be sure of having everything, now, this very day, and it has to be as wonderful as it was when I was little. Otherwise I prefer to die.

ANTIGONE by JEAN ANOUILH (1942)

(Ismene is begging her sister, Antigone, to reconsider her insistence to bury her brother against Creon's orders).

Ismene:

Listen to me, Antigone. I thought about it all night. I'm older than you are. I always think things over and you don't. You are impulsive. You get a notion in your head and you jump up and do the thing straight off. And if it's silly, well, so much the worse for you. Whereas, I think things out. I know it's horrible. And I pity Polynices just as much as you do. But all the same, I sort of see what Uncle Creon means. Uncle Creon is the King. He has to set an example. He is stronger than we are, Antigone. He is the King. And the whole city is with him. Thousands and thousands of them, swarming through all the streets of Thebes. His mob will come running, howling as it runs. A thousand arms will seize our arms. A thousand breaths will breathe into our faces. Like one single pair of eyes, a thousand eyes will stare at us. We'll be driven in a tumbrel through their hatred, through the smell of them and their cruel, roaring laughter. We'll be dragged to the scaffold for torture, surrounded by guards with their idiot faces all bloated, their animal hands clean-washed for the sacrifice, their beefy-eyes squinting as they stare at us. And we'll know that no shrieking and no begging will make them understand that we want to live, for they are like slaves who do exactly as they've been told, without caring about right or wrong. And we shall suffer, we shall feel pain rising in us until it becomes so unbearable that we know it must stop. But it won't stop. It will go on rising and rising, like a screaming voice. Oh, I can't, I can't, Antigone!

COLOMBE by JEAN ANOUILH (1951)

(A scene from Act 3 of Colombe. Madam Alexandra is talking to her son, Julien).

Madame Alexandra:

Have you gone mad? You have sown, my son, now you must reap.

Yes … Your father would always have loved me. That was what frightened me. Why must you always think that love is for eternity? What do you mean when you say "for life"? Our clothes change with the fashions; we move from one house to another; fruit goes rotten; flowers fade … A doctor will tell you that after seven years there isn't a single cell in your body that hasn't changed. We change and decompose from the day we are born, and yet you still go on hoping that love will stay fresh and un-corrupted. Where did you learn to believe such things, you and your father? At school, or in trashy novels? Your heads are so full of second-hand romance that you've forgotten to learn how to live. If your father had started life as I did at thirteen in the Folies Bergeres, he would have known better than to kill himself for love …

You will always be alone – just like your father.

You love her! That is a fact. Another fact of equal importance is that she doesn't love you. Well, what do you want her to do about it? Pretend to love you all her life, just because you love her? Drive yourself mad for fifty years because you think it might help you? Go to bed, and tomorrow go back and play soldiers.

Well … Good Luck. If you don't want to end up like your father, try to get on without asking life to give you quite so much. And forget about "love eternal".

THE LARK by JEAN ANOUILH (1952)

(*From Part One of Anouilh's play about the story of Joan of Arc. Joan explains her voices and subsequent call to battle. She is speaking to Cauchon and Warwick. Joan is wearing man's clothes*).

Joan:

I like remembering the beginning: at home, in the fields, when I was still a little girl looking after the sheep, the first time I heard the Voices, that is what I like to remember … It is after the evening Angelus. I am very small and my hair is still in pigtails. I am sitting in the field, thinking of nothing at all. God is good and keeps me safe and happy, close to my mother and my father and my brother, in the quiet countryside of Domremy, while the English soldiers are looting and burning villages up and down the land. My big sheep-dog is lying with his head in my lap; and suddenly I feel his body ripple and tremble, and a hand seems to have touched my shoulder, though I know no one has touched me.

A great light was filling the shadows. The voice was gentle and grave. I had never heard it before, and all it said to me was: "Be a good and sensible child, and go often to church". But I was good, and I did go to church often, and I showed I was sensible by running away to safety. That was all that happened the first time. And I didn't say anything about it when I got home; but after supper I went back. And then came the second time; the bells were ringing for the noonday Angelus.The light came again, in bright sunlight, but brighter than the sun, and that time I saw him. A man in a white robe with two white wings reaching from the sky to the ground. He didn't tell me his name that day, but later on I found out that he was the blessed St. Michael. "Joan, go to the help of the King of France, and give him back his kingdom. "You will go and search out Robert de Beaudricourt, the Governor. He will give you a suit of clothes to dress you like a man, and he will take you to the Dauphin. St Catherine and St Margaret will protect you. (*She drops to her knees, sobbing*). Please pity me, holy sir! I'm a little girl; I'm happy here alone in the fields. I've never had to be responsible for anything, except my sheep. The Kingdom of

France is far beyond anything I can do. If you will only look at me you will see I am small, and ignorant. Please have pity of me! ... No pity. He had gone already, and there I was, with France on my shoulders.

ACKNOWLEDGEMENTS

Electra by Euripides (410BC)

The Women of Troy by Euripides (415BC)

Andromache by Euripides (425BC)

Medea by Euripides written in 431BC

Lysistrata by Aristophanes (411BC)

Antigone by Sophocles (442BC)

Henry 6th Part 1 by William Shakespeare 1623

Henry 6th Part 3 by William Shakespeare1623

Richard 3rd by William Shakespeare 1597

The Country Wife by William Wycherley 1675

The Way of the World by William Congreve

The Rivals by Richard Brinsley Sheridan 1775

Ivanov by Anton Chekhov 1887

The Seagull by Anton Chekhov 1896

The Wild Duck by Henrik Ibsen 1884

The Lady from the Sea by Henrik Ibsen 1888

Hedda Gabler by Henrik Ibsen 1889

A Doll's House by Henrik Ibsen 1879

Miss Julie by August Strindberg 1888

A Month in the Country by Ivan Turgenev 1855

Hotel Paradiso by Georges Feydeau 1894

Mirandolina by Carlo Goldoni 1751

Tess of the D'Urbervilles by Thomas Hardy 1892

Far from the Madding Crowd by Thomas Hardy 1874

On the Western Circuit by Thomas Hardy 1894

The Picture of Dorian Gray by Oscar Wilde 1890

The Old Curiosity Shop by Charles Dickens 1838

Hard Times by Charles Dickens 1854

Great Expectations by Charles Dickens 1860

Arms and the man by George Bernard Shaw 1894

Fanny's First Play by George Bernard Shaw 1916

Saint Joan by George Bernard Shaw 1923

The Dark Lady of the Sonnets by George Bernard Shaw 1910

Pygmalion by George Bernard Shaw 1912

Mrs Warren's Profession by George Bernard Shaw 1902

Yerma by Federico Garcia Lorca 1934

Dona Rosita, the Spinster by Federico Garcia Lorca 1935

The House of Bernarda Alba by Federico Garcia Lorca 1945

Colombe by Jean Anouilh 1951

Antigone by Jean Anouilh 1942

The Lark by Jean Anouilh 1952

Translations

Electra: The Complete Greek Tragedies, edited by David Greene & Richmond Lattimore, Translated by Emily Townsend Vermeule.

The Women of Troy. Penguin classics and translated by Philip Vellacott.

Andromache. Delphi, The complete work of Euripides. Andromache translated by Edward Coleridge

Medea. Published by Oberon Books and Translated by Alistair Elliot.

Lysistrata. Dover Publications. Translated by Thomas Crofts.

Antigone. Absolute classics. Translated by Declan Donnellan.

Chekhov: Five Plays. Oxford World's Classics. Translated by Ronald Hingley.

Henrik Ibsen: Penguin Classics. Translated by Una Ellis-Fermor.

August Strindberg: Open University. Translated by Michael Meyer.

Carlo Goldoni: Oxford University Press. Translated by Eleanor & Herbert Farjeon.

Georges Feydeau. The Drama Library. Adapted by Peter Glenville.

Federico Garcia Lorca: Oxford World's Classics. Translated by John Edmunds.

Jean Anouilh: Methuen. Antigone: Translated by Barbara Bray. Colombe: Translated by Lois Kronenburg.

ABOUT THE AUTHOR

Kim Gilbert trained for three years as a professional actress at the Guildford School of Acting, studied for an LGSM at Guildhall School of Music and Drama and an English degree at the Open University. She has been acting, teaching and directing plays and musical productions for more than 35 years. She has experience in a wide range of theatre, TV and voiceover work. She has a First-class Honours degree in English and has taught English and Drama in many top schools in the country. Kim has examined for Lamda for a number of years and has been running Dramatic Arts Studio for 11 years, a private drama studio which specialises in developing excellence in all forms of performance and communication.

www.dramaticartsstudio.com

Other Books by the same author:

Shakespeare Scenes

Monologues for young female actors
Monologues for young adult female actors
Duologues for female actors
Monologues for young male actors

Chekhov Scenes

Monologues & Duologues for women
Monologues for Male Actors

Scenes from Oscar Wilde

Monologues & Duologues for female actors
Monologues for male actors
Duologues for male & female actors

Available from Amazon Bookstore

"Thanks for reading! If you enjoyed this book or found it useful, I'd be very grateful if you'd post a short review on Amazon. Your support really does make a difference and I read all the reviews personally so I can get your feedback and make this book even better.

Thanks again for your support!"